OUT OF THE RUBBLE

Cover design by Marjan Gerritze and Trikolesh Mukherjee

For Phyllis, my adopted mother

Out of the Rubble

Pauletta J. Edwards

Published in 1999 by
Pauletta J. Edwards
Pump Cottage
Pulteney Gardens
Bath
BA2 4JF

Design and typesetting by
EX LIBRIS PRESS
1 The Shambles
Bradford on Avon
Wiltshire

Printed in Britain by
Cromwell Press
Trowbridge
Wiltshire

ISBN 0 9534787 0 X

CONTENTS

Acknowledgements

I offer my warmest thanks and gratitude to all those who have read and commented upon the book and encouraged me throughout the writing of it.

I wish to thank particularly: Professor Jean La Fontaine for giving detailed and helpful advice on the first draft; Phillipa Brewster, Editor for the Literary Consultancy in London, for reading the first two drafts and offering invaluable advice and considerable help with the editing of the book; Jenny Kenrick of the Tavistock Centre, London, for her advice and help on the road to publication; Tessa Dowding, friend and helper, who has processed and reprocessed draft after draft and written dozens of letters with great speed and imperturbable good humour; last but very much not least Phyllis, my adopted mother, who has weathered my highs and lows while writing and publishing the book with unruffled serenity.

Foreword

This is a harrowing story but it is also full of hope. It shows in the most painful detail what it felt like to be abandoned when only 18 months old and, throughout a loveless upbringing in a children's home, to have no value as a human being. At its darkest it is a story of cruelty to children, both emotional and physical, at best a catalogue of exploitation and cold, harsh treatment by a Christian group who were named, with bitter irony, the Sisters of Mercy. Yet it is also a moving account of how one of these children was helped through the long healing process that made her into a loving, mature woman. It would be easy to say: "Well things are better now", but recent cases have shown that the inhumanity of adults to children is still a threat to those most vulnerable beings. The hope held out by this book lies in its message, set out with painful honesty, that with patience, perseverance and love these damaged children can be healed.

Professor J.S. La Fontaine

INTRODUCTION

This is my story - the story of "how it was for me". I have made no attempt to be objective. There is no analysis - only self-analysis - or learned psychological reference. Too much of either would take away from "how it was for me". I leave the reader to do the analysing and referencing. For all of us, how we interpret a situation is how it is - for us. To say: "That isn't really what I meant" is irrelevant.

For seventeen and a half years I had lived in The Haven, in a state of fear and anger, desperation and desolation and a deep, deep longing. Over all this had hung a huge cloud of bewilderment and confusion. It had become darker as I passed from childhood to adolescence and grew in understanding. This cloud arose from the dichotomy between what Sisters of Mercy said and did when they were communing with their God and what they said and did when they were looking after little children. The two parts of this frightening whole never did and never have become reconciled for me; for The Haven was a Children's Home and it was run by the Sisters of Mercy.

The Haven was called The Orphanage of Pity at first. It had been opened in 1850, only sixteen years after the Poor Law Amendment Act of 1834. This Act decreed that life in Workhouses and similar institutions should be made so unpleasant that people would rather stay outside if possible. Whether the cruelty and ignominy sanctioned by this Act was meant to apply to Children's Homes or not, it certainly did to ours. It also did and has to others, as Peter Lennon's article in the Guardian of March 1996 shows.

For orphans, waifs and strays there was no choice. We were dumped, like pieces of junk, wherever a place in an Orphanage could be found. Forsaken by parents, abandoned on doorsteps or left in the gutter - as we were often told we were - we huddled together seeking a love and warmth which didn't exist.

We were the rubbish, the rubble of life.

This book is about the damage done to me in the rubble heap; its extent and depth and my reactions to it. I have written as honestly as possible, though it hasn't always been easy to tell the truth but had I not done so there would be no point to the book. I have written it in such a way that the reader can come with me; feel how and where the psychological damage came from and how it affected my life; learn how healing took place - the winning, the losing, the fears and the joys; the despair and the hope as they happened and as they gradually broke down my defensive front; how Phyllis (my adopted mother) managed to pull me out of the rubble and slowly and carefully put me back together again. It is about the trauma and hurt inflicted, often unwittingly, by both my adopted mother and me during the restoration period and about the degree to which repair was possible in my case

I don't say that this is how everyone in the rubble or from it feels and reacts. What the book is saying is: Look under the surface for what is hidden, often very, very deeply, as it was with me.

To pull someone damaged almost beyond salvaging out of the rubble of life into love, hope and happiness requires loyalty; steadfastness; the ability and the willingness to withstand the emotional manifestations of the pain, the anger and the fear of betrayal as learning and healing take place; the insight to see the love of a frightened child trying to respond beneath the tough, bolshie, "don't care" or prickly front. Above all, the total commitment to spend years of loving and caring, waiting for the breakthrough; believing there will be one.

In my adopted mother I found all these things.

I hope the book will help all those who come in contact with or care for all of us who have been pulled out of the rubble, or more sadly, those who are still in it.

Pauletta J. Edwards

PHYLLIS'S THOUGHTS
(My adopted mother)

As we grow older, do we grow wiser? Perhaps wisdom comes in flashes of self knowledge - I am sure I am the better for seeing myself through the eyes of a biographer!

This story, of the two of us, Pauletta and I, learning to live together, youth and age, is really two stories - the one motherless, starved of love, learning to be a daugher and the other finding how to be a mother, to realise the daughter's needs and gifts.

In this process we have blundered at times, been unwittingly hurtful; but with every new insight came joy and a clearer vision of the other's worth. We are more rounded, purposeful characters from the experience we have shared. In a relationship where there is love and trust, life is joyful despite its difficulties.

If there were to be a next-time round, how much more sensitive to an adopted daughter's wants and fears I would surely be! Perhaps then as we passed from stage to stage I would sometimes see two daughters not one - the efficient, confident, successful academic alongside the frightened child hiding from the world.

May the telling of this story of a relationship, so long and difficult but ultimately so warm and fulfilling, bring hope and help to those others young and old who need time and tenderness to come from aloneness to a fuller life as well as to their adoptive families who must make the journey with them and be gladdened by it.

ACT 1

RESPECTABLE DEVILS

"The devil's most devilish when respectable."

Elizabeth Barrett Browning;

Aurora Leigh, bk vi.

Chapter 1

Finding My Feet

I was tossed onto the heap of rubble when I was about 18 months old; just another unwanted brat. I landed in the Orphanage of Pity in Wiltshire.

I was taken there by Miss Russell, a Christian Moral Welfare worker, who ran a Home in the Midlands for single mothers. She knew my father, who lived in the same town as her, and in those days there was much less formality involved in putting children into Care.

When I reached the Orphanage in the mid-thirties there were thirty of us, though over the years the numbers ranged from twenty to thirty. It was for girls only, as was the norm in institutions of any kind until comparatively recently, though we had the occasional infant boy for a short time. Ages ranged from a few months to school-leaving age, which was in those days fourteen or, later, fifteen and the girls then left the Orphanage. Many of them went into domestic service, for which we were more than adequately trained, or became nannies or whatever.

The Orphanage was run by two of the Sisters of Mercy from the Convent, which was about a quarter of a mile away. These Sisters were changed quite often in my early years but when I was first put in the Orphanage they were Sisters Margaret Mary and Agatha - known to us as Mouldy Cheese and Aggy Ragbag.

When I arrived I was the youngest child and I was not very talkative; in fact, I confined myself to one word: NO. It was said that I was tongue-tied but when, apparently, our Family Doctor snipped the tongue-tie I began chattering like a magpie. For the Sisters this was a mixed blessing; relief at knowing that I could talk mingled with the exhaustion of having to listen to me.

I loved words and phrases and picked them up very quickly. One day, when I was about two years old, I was sitting in my high chair, its back against the kitchen window-sill. The sill was seven inches wide and three foot off the ground. Mouldy Cheese was cooking lunch and my: "What's that? What are you doing? Why, why, why?" was driving her mad. Eventually she said: "Oh, for Heavens' sake be quiet." I obeyed. In fact, I was so quiet that Mouldy Cheese, who was working at the kitchen range in front of me, became suspicious and she turned towards me. "Whatever are you doing?" she cried, crossing the kitchen at speed. "Ssh," I whispered, "I'm being quiet." I was halfway along the windowsill.

The Sisters observed two depths of silence: the Greater Silence, which lasted from after Compline, the last Office (prayer session) of the day, until after Holy Communion at 6.30 a.m., the following morning. During this period, Absolute Silence was observed except in the most urgent of circumstances. The Lesser Silence governed the rest of the twenty-four hours and during those hours the Sisters only spoke when necessary. This probably explains why we seldom talked to the Sisters except on official business, though they almost certainly had some leeway when looking after us. As a little girl I quite often answered to "What are you doing?" with "I'm being quiet," when I suspected that the real answer wouldn't be acceptable. It never worked, of course. My inability to speak was a short-lived difficulty but I had other disabilities which led to many problems. I was hammer-toed, short-sighted and night-blind, with a squint in the left eye.

The short sight was discovered quite early on. I was in my high chair, playing with a pile of cigarette cards when I suddenly threw them all on the floor so I was put down amongst them to pick them all up again. This I did by picking each one up and scrutinising it about an inch away from my eye, murmuring to Aggy Ragbag as I put each one on the pile: " S'ard work." It must have been soon after this that I was given spectacles. They were metal ones and I quickly grew out of each pair. As the Orphanage was poor, the spectacles couldn't always be replaced as soon as was comfortable and my early childhood was overlaid with the misery of sore ears and nose.

My high chair, which was in the kitchen, was a great vantage point for watching what went on and the kitchen was where visitors were often given a cup of tea. I sometimes passed on the knowledge I had gleaned - and not always at the right time.

The Sisters used to make plum jam; oceans of it to last the year. It was full of stones and, for some reason, it very often crystallised. The usual method of dealing with this was to break the jar as this was the only way of getting the jam out. The kitchen floor was tiled so it was just right for breaking jars. One day a visitor arrived and was treated to tea and toast with plum jam,. I told the visitor, very conversationally, that "S't'r Agatha broke a jam jar." Aggy Ragbag was not best pleased at having to explain to the visitor what I meant.

About this time I must have been too active to keep in a high chair. Aggy Ragbag told me years later that I was "headstrong and not over-obedient" so life could not have been easy for the Sisters once I was mobile. Nor did it help when Shirley came to the Orphanage. Shirley was about my own age and we had great fun inventing new games which were seldom approved of by the Sisters so we were both constantly in hot water.

Chapter 2

Learning The Ropes

"The Quality of Mercy is not strained...."
                                    Merchant of Venice, Act IV Scene 1.

Rules, rules, rules. Every step we took was governed by some regulation or other. It was like walking through a minefield and I soon learned to do nothing unless I was told to or unless I knew that it was safe to do it. We sometimes broke the rules, of course,, even though we knew that punishment - and often severe punishment - would surely follow if we were caught. More frightening, though, were the rules we broke because we never even knew that they existed - especially during the learning period.

So many regulations applied to using the lavatory, for example. On Saturdays or during the holidays we were sent out into the garden if it were fine. Once out, we were not allowed back into the house until we were told we could go in - not even to spend a penny and that often caused a real problem. At the first telltale sign of discomfort we would put a hand between our legs and press hard to stifle the urge to pass water. Sometimes we were lucky and got away with it unseen. More often, the Sister would call from one of the windows: "So-and-so, don't "hold" yourself. Leave your "in between" alone, you dirty little thing." It was years before I found out that that wasn't the proper word or why the Sisters thought it was "dirty" and "disgusting". Without knowing why, I began to be embarrassed about my "in-between."

One day, quite by chance, I discovered a more discreet way. We were playing marbles, using small stones in the absence of marbles, for which we "coopied down." In other words, we squatted down, like milkmaids on their low stools, or "copies" - pronounced "coopy". I used to sit on my heel and, on the day of revelation, I found that this blocked the sensation to pass water. I never told any of the other girls because, really, it was the same as "holding" myself but from then on "coopying" was my salvation, especially as we were often out in the garden for an hour or more. Sometimes, especially in high summer, we went out into the garden of our own accord and on those occasions we could go back into the lavatory. It was only on the formally compulsory occasions that we weren't allowed back in; days when it was too cold for us to want to go out or when we were too absorbed in an indoor game.

Quite the worst regulation, though, was not being allowed to use the lavatory at night. The night is a very long time, particularly when trying to cope with a full bladder. Occasionally, my Big Girl, Barbara, would creep with me to the lavatory and then I learned the true meaning of Absolute Silence. We became Big Girls when we were 11 years old and then we were allotted a Little Girl to look after.

The night came when the most dreaded thing happened. I was four years old; too young to sneak to the lavatory by myself, too night-blind to do so anyway and no longer in the same dormitory as my Big Girl. I wet the bed; not just a little dampness on the sheet but soaking sheets and a very wet mattress as well. Wetting the bed was a serious offence and there was never any chance of being let off the consequences, even in those early years when corporal punishment was confined to spanking.

Every morning, when we were all dressed, we assembled on the landing and filed down to Chapel for morning prayers. On the morning of my disgrace, Mouldy Cheese sat down on the big chest on the landing and, in front of all the other girls she told me, at length, what a horrid little girl I was. She then put me over her knee, pulled down my knickers and gave me my first remembered, very long and painful spanking. The pain was as nothing compared to the ignominy of being spanked in public and having my bottom exposed. We were never allowed to show our nether regions when we were getting dressed or undressed; we always had to have our nighties on when we took off or put on our knickers. Thus, no-one ever saw our bottoms unless we were being punished or having a bath and I grew to hate being naked because of its association with pain and humiliation.

Talking in the dormitory after we had gone to bed, while not being so heinous a crime as wetting the bed, was just as punishable. We might be spanked or we might be sent downstairs to the laundry or kitchen to stand behind the door. This was not quite as mild a punishment as it might seem because, for one thing, standing still behind a door for an hour or more is both tiring and boring. For another, the Orphanage was overrun with cockroaches which came out at night. They were not wiped out as they should have been by the DDT powder which was sprinkled round the floors at night and they just walked over any bare feet in their path.

Other aspects of our life were controlled by instilling behaviour patterns into us for character building rather than by regulation, though there seemed to be very little difference between the two. "Get up. You're not hurt. Go on playing," one of the Sisters would call out of the window if we fell over. We would fight back the tears, stop rubbing our heads or inspecting our bleeding knees and go back to the game. "What are you crying for? Cry Baby Bunting," would stop the tears, springing to our eyes from whatever cause; like another girl taking away our plaything from us or a visiting mother leaving, murmuring promises to her daughter which she would never keep. I soon learned not to cry or complain of hurt, even when I was bullied.

We all learned to bully each other or were spiteful on occasion; we took our cue in this from the Sisters. When the Sisters said: "Cry Baby Bunting" we all sang it in full at the weeping child. If someone cried because she was hurt we would chant:

> Cowardy, cowardy custard
> Give her a bowl of mustard.

This in spite of the fact that it might be our turn next. We sucked up to the Sisters rather than sympathising with the sufferer in case we got a dose of the same medicine. If any of us had something wrong with us or had a bad habit, this might be castigated in public and the rest of us would take it up. For example, I bit my nails down to the quick and chewed the skin off my knuckles. When we were playing circle games - like The Farmer's in his Den - where everyone holds hands and walks round in a circle, Sister might suddenly pick on me. "Ugh," she would say, "those horrible bitten nails. I don't know how anyone can bear to hold your hand." The two children who had been holding my hands quite peaceably up to that point would drop them in revulsion. "Ugh," they would say in imitation, "how horrible." I would walk round with the others, arms at my sides, pretending I didn't care and gradually, surreptitiously, the girls either side of me would take my hands again.

We had to eat everything on our plates, regardless of its condition or whether it agreed with us or not. When any of us turned up our noses at slightly "off" meat, baulked at slimy, overcooked boiled marrow or refused something which gave us diarrhoea, we took our plate to the kitchen and sat for hours retching over the congealed mess.

Once when I was in bed recovering from a childhood ailment, the soggy marrow was on the menu. As no-one was about I put it in the waste paper basket in the bedroom. It was a real wickerwork one and the fluid ran out of the bottom and made a puddle on the linoleum floor. When the Sister came up to see how I was getting on the puddle on the floor and the contents of the wastepaper basket told her. She spanked me hard, hauled me out of bed and put me beside the basket. "Eat it." she commanded. There were little bits of hair from the basket stuck on the marrow but I had no choice but to eat it. I tried hard to swallow it but my throat closed and I was sick into the basket. Sister was furious. She pushed my face into the basket, then she spanked me even harder and dumped me back on my bed. I smelt awful. After that, I always ate my food.

The main thing wrong with the food was that there was never enough of it. We were chronically hungry and as thin as scarecrows. We were not allowed to help ourselves outside of mealtimes and that would not have been easy in any case. The pantry was in the kitchen and, for most of the day, so was one of the Sisters. Helping ourselves was   stealing and carried a stern penalty

By the age of five years I had learnt what I must do and was not allowed to do; I was learning to be afraid and to fall into line; I was developing a distorted sense of right and wrong and I was thoroughly and   completely   institutionalised.

Chapter 3

Government

"With how little wisdom ... governed ..."

Oxenstierna: Letter to his Son.

The two Sisters who looked after us actually spent very little time together with us. Each day they both spent a few hours in the Convent. At 6 a.m. one Sister would go "down" to the Convent - the road to it was downhill. The Sister would attend Holy Communion in the Convent chapel at 6.30 a.m., followed by breakfast with the other Sisters. She would then report to the Reverend Mother and pick up any post. About mid-morning she would come "up" to the Orphanage. Both Sisters would be together till 4 p.m. then the other Sister would go "down" to tea and Vespers at 6 p.m. She also reported to the Reverend Mother and collected any letters which came by second post, together with any instructions or information. The Sisters took it in turns to be "up" or "down" in the mornings and evenings and this meant that there was only one Sister with us for much of the day.

From 2 p.m. - 3 p.m., when we were at school, both Sisters would go "down" for the Recreation Hour. This was passed in the Recreation Room, where the Sisters were allowed to break the Lesser Silence and talk freely to each other. Or reasonably freely, for some topics were taboo - like sex or one's own ailments.

My friend Shirley only stayed at the Orphanage for a year and I was the youngest by about two years after she left. All the other children were at school. The Sisters would sometimes take me "down" with them for Recreation and I have snapshot memories of those hours.

In the Recreation Room was a large table with a jigsaw on it. Several Sisters would be working at it and I would be allowed to help. I loved it. I think the Sisters must have put pieces near me which fitted into the corner where I was because I was often able to fit a piece into the jigsaw. Some of the Sisters were teachers and I think they used the time to teach me because I could sometimes put them right when they misplaced a piece. The Sister concerned would ask me to put it in the right place and I would helpfully show her where it went. These hours gave me a passion for jigsaw puzzles, which I still have.

These visits to the Recreation Room didn't happen often enough for my liking. I was more likely to be taken by a woman called Miss Burgess to her home, which was a short distance from the Orphanage. I hated those days, for her family had a wireless (radio) and I was mortally afraid of the wireless. I had three phobias in those early years; I was terrified of birds, dogs and the disembodied voice coming out of the wireless.

Birds I learned to tolerate; dogs I could cope with if I could keep someone between the dog and me; but the voice from the wireless was much more menacing because it was unseen and wouldn't go away. I would scream until somebody stopped me with a heavy hand, then I would stare at the wireless in fascinated horror.

Every year the Sisters had a Chapter Meeting, when many Sisters' jobs were changed. Some went to the Tropical Mission Field, some to Branch Houses and very often- until I was 12 years old - one or both Sisters at the Orphanage were replaced. If an Orphanage Sister were changed it was highly unsettling for us and we showed it.

We had to learn what kind of person the new Sister was, how she would react in a given situation, how much patience she had and so on. If only one Sister were replaced, little was altered in our daily routine. The resident Sister would teach the newcomer what to do and how to do it and when they were both "up" we were reasonably well-behaved. When the new Sister was "up" on her own, though, it was a different story. Unsettled as we were, we would be naughtier than usual and test her to find out where the red light was. If she were weak or tried to operate outside the authoritarianism in which we were steeped she soon realised her mistake. When she was "up" she had a very bad time until she had discovered how to deal with us. Punishments might be meted out when the other Sister came "up" but they didn't make much difference. They were part of life and hardly changed our behaviour at all. Usually the new Sister would get the message and stop sparing the rod while the other was applying it in full force. Or, alternatively, the newcomer might be in complete agreement with such a regime from the start, in which case it wasn't long before we knew it. Sometimes the new Sister never saw the point and went on trying to be kind. If so, she would be replaced by someone with more experience and everything then returned to normal.

When there was a complete change of Government and both Sisters were replaced, there was a radical change in our lives, which led to general mayhem. Not only did we children have to contend with two totally new personalities; we also had to adjust to the whole pattern of our lives being altered. The red lights were in different places, the goalposts moved about all over the place and we went out of control. This double-change happened twice during my time in the Orphanage; once when I was five years old and once when I was twelve. At five years I was really too young to understand and the girls were more settled and docile then so we weathered the change in relative calm. When I was twelve years old it was quite a different story. By that time girls were staying on a more short-term basis and we were all the more unsettled because of it.

Firstly, a new County Children's Home had been built and the number of children at The Haven was declining. Secondly, because of the introduction of the Welfare State less money was being donated to The Haven. Consequently, we had often only just got to know new girls before they were off home or elsewhere so we had less stability, even in our own ranks.

I had passed the Scholarship (11+) and had been at the Grammar School for only a year at the time of the change so I was already having to get used to a fundamental difference in my way of life. My fellow-inmates at the Orphanage all went together to the local Secondary Modern school; I went by myself by train to school. I had homework to do; I played games after school hours and so on. The other Big Girls walked to school together; some were in the same classes; they didn't have homework; they didn't stay after school so I was trying to come to terms with being different and alone. When both Sisters were changed at the end of October, 1947 we blew our fuses.

Normally we weren't allowed to go out anywhere unless we were escorted, except on errands. My going to school alone was already a novel departure from that. We never visited friends after school or had them visit us so once school was over and during the holidays we were completely cut off from our schoolmates.

After the two-Sister change, four of us went on the rampage and it lasted from the end of November to the middle of January. We were already making the life of one of the new Sisters a living hell. Sister Eleanor either didn't know about or didn't believe in authoritarianism and I don't think she knew what a red light was. Poor Sister Eleanor. We soon taught her. We taunted her; we played her up; we were totally disobedient and when she was "up" she must have suffered unremitting misery. If she prayed to God for help He obviously wasn't listening. Sister Penelope, the other Sister and in charge, did her best to bring us back under control but without any success. Sister Eleanor had taken the lid off our frustrations, our fear, our desperation and our misery just by trying to be kind and we had run amok.

Three of the girls quite often met me at the station when I came home from school and we went into town and made whoopee, using money stolen by one of the other three. We stayed out till late at night, going to the pictures or doing whatever else took our fancy. When we got back to the Orphanage we climbed through the chapel window which Rosie, one of the other Big Girls, had left unlatched for us. Punishment was pointless. We had the bit between our teeth and were quite unmanageable.

On a day when the girls didn't meet me, I got back to the Orphanage to find that Sister Annette had returned. Sister Annette had been with us before. She had come back as assistant to Sister Penelope in place of Sister Eleanor and she knew things about control which Sister Penelope did not. They were denigration and malice. Dear Sister Eleanor would never have learnt or used them and she had not remembered that Sisters of Mercy should hold themselves at a distance emotionally.

Sister Annette brought me sharply back into line that day. Children in Orphanages were not to be treated with gentleness; they could not handle it and were not worthy of it. They had to be controlled with a rod of iron. Hadn't we proved that over the last few weeks in our thoroughly bad behaviour? Hadn't we shown it when Sister Eleanor had tried to relax discipline and had ("mistakenly" understood) tried to be kind to us? (Even the observance of Christmas had gone by the board because we were still creating mayhem in spite of the Season of Goodwill.)

Sister Annette had a razor-sharp tongue which could cut us to ribbons. We avoided it at all costs if we could. When she finally sent me to bed, I went. Secretly, I was glad that the mayhem was over. For one thing, it being winter, my night-blindness had prevented me from entirely enjoying the escapades. For another, my school-work was suffering and I had to get back on an even keel.

Chapter 4

Work and Play

Who sweeps a room as for Thy Laws...
(Hymn: Teach Me My God and King)

With only two Sisters running the Orphanage they had no time for cleaning. Besides, with twenty or more children, there were enough of us to do it. Apart from that, in those days it was taken for granted that in such places the inmates did the housework. The Sister in charge did the paperwork and cooked the lunch, though we children prepared the vegetables. The other Sister did some of the "big" ironing - sheets, for example - and made out the bath and work rotas.

I can't remember how often we changed jobs but it was probably once a week. What I do remember is trying to keep in favour so that we got a "nice" job. The dining room I always thought of as a "nice" chore and even before I was old enough to be able to do it I coveted it. The dining room had two large tables which held us all more or less comfortably depending on how many of us there were. Those tables shone like glass and if there were flowers on them, from Harvest Festival donations, they were clearly reflected in the surface. The tables were kept like this by whoever's job it was to clean the dining room; they were polished thoroughly every Saturday and rubbed hard with a polishing cloth after meals every day. Whatever job we had, it had to be done as perfectly as possible or we did it again. We soon learnt that it was never worth trying to skimp even the smallest part of any task and we were scrupulously thorough in all things.

We started cleaning at a very early age and our first chore, at

28

four or five years old, was to "pick the mats." There were three of these, in the hall, and we had to remove every scrap of fluff or other dirt every morning. As we grew older we graduated to proper work. We all had chores to do every morning before we went to school; getting the small children up; seeing that all our beds were made properly; a quick but thorough sweeping and dusting of the dormitories, the chapel, the dining room, the kitchen, cloakrooms, and so on. The kitchen range, the stove which took the chill off the playroom and the parlour grate all had to be raked out and "made up." The stove and range were filled with anthracite and in the parlour the fire had to be laid and lit. By the time we were twelve years old most of us were dabhands at lighting fires and stoking boilers.

At lunch time we just cleaned the dining room and laid up for tea, cut and "scraped" the bread for tea with margarine or butter and did the washing up. The kitchen had to be cleaned after each meal and the girl in charge of stoves and fires "made them up" and filled the coal scuttles. In the evenings there were extra jobs, like preparing the vegetables for next day's lunch, cutting and spreading the bread for breakfast, putting the little ones to bed and cleaning the shoes. Larking about while working was not allowed and was an indictable offence. On one occasion I was cleaning the shoes with a girl called Jessica and we had lined up about 25 pairs ready in front of us. Jessica was "putting (the polish) on" and I was "taking off". Jessica was trying to dab my nose with polish and we got too noisy in our merry-making: "Ssh!" whispered Jessica suddenly but it was already too late. Sister Annette had come almost silently into the backhouse. She picked up a Big Girl's shoe and, since I was nearest, belaboured me about the head with it. I just threw my arms over my head and waited for it to stop. Sister Annette then turned to do the same to Jessica but Jessica had slid to the end of the bench we were sitting on. She already had a shoe in her hand and she began systematically to throw shoe after shoe at Sister Annette. Jessica had an excellent aim and she seldom missed the target, even as Sister Annette backed towards the door. After that we cleaned the shoes in subdued silence and when Sister Penelope came "up" after Vespers Jessica got a good thrashing. Playing the fool was never a good idea.

Monday morning was washing day for the "smalls"- underwear and pinafores. We always got up at 5.45 a.m. so fitting in the washing before school wasn't difficult and four girls saw it through in no time. We had an old-fashioned copper and that was filled and lit. Then boilable clothes were boiled and woolly vests and socks were washed in one of the three large sinks. One girl washed, one did the first rinse, one the second rinse and one mangled. The mangle was a large table-top, with big rollers and a heavy wheel to turn the rollers. In summer the washing was hung up outside but in winter there were two large, four-railed pulleys in the kitchen to hang it on. "Big" washing, like sheets and towels, was done on Saturday.

Saturday was also Big Cleaning Day and the Orphanage was cleaned, every nook and cranny, from top to bottom. Floors were polished or scrubbed; every ledge, however minute, was dusted; windows were cleaned and brass door knobs shined into brilliance. The front doorsteps were scrubbed, the brass bell-pull cleaned and the plaque telling the world that this was the Orphanage of Pity was carefully washed. The kitchen range was cleaned with blacklead and the wide steel edgings scoured with emery paper. The chapel was cleaned, the benches and the brass candlesticks polished, the frontal and dossal of the altar changed in keeping with the Christian Calendar and the altar cloth washed. The Big Washing was done and hung on the lines outside and we struggled through the ironing from Monday's wash with two old-fashioned irons. One iron stood on the kitchen range while the other one was in use. To find out if the iron was hot enough we spat on it and if the spit formed spluttering globules and slid off, it was all right to use. In 1950 someone gave us an electric iron, which made the ironing much quicker and much less dangerous for us children.

I liked any job which involved polishing. I loved the shine on everything and the smell of Mansion polish. I liked particularly the cold, clear brightness of polished brass, though I couldn't stand the smell of Brasso. On the other hand, I loathed any chore which involved slopping about in water - scrubbing floors, washing clothes or cleaning the yard - because my clothes got wet and stayed uncomfortable for hours.

By lunch-time the whole house was spick and span. We certainly learned "to toil and not to seek for rest". Some jobs took less time than others and those lucky girls who had finished could go to play.

In the garden we played Donkey or two, three or four-ball. These games involved throwing each ball in turn against the wall in continuous and unbroken succession. With the first ball of each sequence we followed an intricate pattern of manoeuvres: for instance, we threw the first ball overarm; (the rest were always underarm;) bounced it under one knee; put an arm round our waist and threw the ball at the wall and so on. The pattern was always the same whether two, three or four-ball. Two was easy; three more difficult but to juggle four balls and include the first-ball manoeuvres was quite a feat. Once a ball was dropped the player was "out" and went to the back of the queue. I can't remember how we got old tennis balls or the spongy, bouncy ones which existed then. They somehow just appeared, probably donated when they were too bald for tennis or had too many bites out of the sponge. So long as a tennis ball wasn't split it was all right for ball-juggling games. When it was split we used it for Piggy in the Middle. We sometimes played Piggy in The Middle in the playroom, which was forbidden, understandably, because of the windows. We usually stopped when a Big Girl told us to but if we didn't like the Big Girl we took our time stopping.

One day Martha, who wasn't popular with any of us, told us roughly and repeatedly to stop or she would tell Sister and suddenly, our frustration, which was never far below the surface, broke out. There were five of us playing; two at each end and a "piggy". We threw the ball to each other while Martha tried to catch it. She got crosser and crosser and eventually stamped off to report us. We were all punished but that didn't matter. We had done Martha in the eye and we were mightily pleased with ourselves. As Big Girls got older they sometimes got to be a bit like the Sisters. Martha had.

With so many of us we could play exciting games like off-ground touch, rounders, hopscotch and communal skipping. It was mainly in rounders that we learned to "Get up. You aren't hurt." though it did happen in other games. For hopscotch we marked out the squares with a chunk of chalky stone we brought back from the

Downs when we went for a walk. Communal skipping was great fun. A girl at either end would turn a long piece of rope and six or seven of us would jump the rope together, chanting:

> *All in together, girls,*
> *This fine weather, girls;*
> *I saw Esau*
> *Sitting on a seesaw.*

Anyone who didn't clear the rope was "out". Or we would jump in at one end and gradually move along and out of the other end so that we made a continuous moving file. The best game by far, though, was off-ground touch. One girl would be "on it" - the catcher; she would have to touch one of us on the ground as we ran from perch to perch. We would all run about, dodging the catcher and getting off-ground if she got too near. Not all perches were easy; sometimes we had to cling to a washing-line post or a window sill. Whoever got "touched" was "on it" - or just "it". We "dipped" at the start of any game to choose who would be the catcher - when the game required it. That meant counting round the ring of girls, pointing at each one to the rhythm of a ditty. There were several of these. One was:

> *Dip, dip, dip,*
> *My little ship,*
> *Sailing on the water*
> *Like a cup and saucer.*
> *Who d'you think is "it"?*

Whoever the pointing finger stopped at would be "it".

One perch gave us an idea for another game. There was a flagstone path running the length of the garden - more a yard really. Most of it was an asphalt area 15 foot x 30 foot with the path running alongside it. The playroom ran halfway along the other side of the path and at the end of the playroom was a scruffy bit of turf where there was a rabbit run. The rabbits (we had two) burrowed and burrowed so the run was moved round until the whole patch was mostly bits of burrow. One of the Big Girls then rolled it flat with a large roller. The roller was quite a heavy one to push, even for a Big Girl and it stood on the path next to the patch of turf. This roller made a good, though rather precarious perch for off-ground touch. If whoever was "it" was too close and we had to jump on the roller quickly, the jump started it rolling slightly because the path sloped just a bit downhill. When that happened we either had to balance by "walking" a couple of steps on it or jump off fast. Just as most children like games with an element of danger, so did we. One of us discovered that if we "walked", with our feet a tiny bit towards the back of the roller, and pushed hard with our feet, we could start it rolling. After the first few steps the roller gained momentum and didn't need much pushing after that. It was then just a matter of keeping our balance and "running" backwards to keep the momentum going. When we reached the end of the path we jumped off before the roller bumped into the wall and pulled the roller back for the next in line.

Hide-and-seek was another favourite and the choice of hiding place was sometimes perilous. One girl, Sybil, found one by climbing up on the backhouse roof. This roof was sloping, with its lower edge three feet from the ground and it was made of stout, rounded wooden braces, with glass between. Whether Sybil slipped or unwisely stepped on the glass I don't know but it shattered and Sybil fell, with a leg either side of a brace. She was rushed to hospital, bleeding from nasty cuts on both legs. A veto was put on that hiding place but it wasn't necessary. None of us would have ever dared to use it again.

The most dangerous and very exciting game was "last across", played during World War II. Our town was HQ for many Army and RAF units, American and Canadian as well as British. Their convoys were an everyday event going past our primary school and the Orphanage, which were both in the same street. The road ran almost straight from the Orphanage to the school but at the school it swung round a long, curving bend, blind to us as we walked to school. The convoys came round this corner, often when we were going to morning school. The army lorries moved fairly slowly up our road and the idea was not to be last across the road while running between the lorries. The gaps between the lorries were just long enough to dash through the space so long as we chose the right moment. One day a girl called Ursula left it too late and ran behind what proved to be the last lorry. We were nearly at the school by this time and a police car swept round the bend. Luckily the car wasn't travelling very fast when it knocked poor Ursula over and all she got was a broken leg but it frightened us enough to put paid to the game.

If it was raining we played board games inside; ludo, housey housey (now called Bingo) and snakes and ladders. Or we played cards. Some girls had dolls and played Mums and Dads with them. I didn't; I didn't know how and I was bored by it. Miss Russell had given me a doll but I never played with it; I would much rather do a jigsaw. Many of the children came to the Orphanage when they were already a few years old and some left after a short time, maybe a few months, maybe a couple of years, so the playmate population was always changing.

On Saturday afternoons and most days during holidays we went for long walks, often more than five miles. Babies didn't often come because walks were usually across country or up on the Wiltshire Downs and were wholly unsuitable for pushchairs. Toddlers, once they could walk properly and well did go - and they went on their feet most of the way. Those walks were hard on little legs at first, though they grew sturdy very quickly. In my earliest years I apparently had a habit of choosing a likely customer and gazing up at him with tears running silently down my cheeks and my feet dragging. The chosen man would usually offer to carry me and sometimes the offer was accepted but more often he was told that I was just trying it on. I expect I was some of the time, though there must have been times when my legs were screaming for mercy until they got used to the long tramps.

I loved those walks. Once off the road we could "break rank"; the crocodile broke up and we could do what we liked, within reason, though we had to stay near the Sister who was with us. We picked bluebells, primroses, wood anemones and ox-eye daisies for the Chapel and dining room. We found the first cowslips or harebells and ran up hill and down dale. I regret now that we weren't taught the history of the places where we walked as the area was steeped in Anglo-Saxon and Roman history and learning about it would have made the walks even richer. However, the outings were full of natural history, much of which we picked up for ourselves, though sometimes we were taught. For example, Sister Maria, from the Convent, always used to take us for a walk after the Three-Hour service on Good Friday and we went to the Downs to look for primroses and violets on the lower wooded slopes. Sister Maria, who I think was short sighted like me, carried a magnifying glass and she would show us the wonder of flowers. We would look through the glass into the centre of delicate violets, primroses and other plants and for me, with my poor sight, it was magic.

Picnics were a common feature of holidays but I was always apprehensive about them and I never really enjoyed them because of the tension. Something had almost always been forgotten in packing the picnic or was left behind at the end and the culprit was always sent to get it, however far. We often went blackberrying in the summer holidays and, with so many of us, we picked enormous quantities. These were made into jam and on the days when we picked we had apple and blackberry tart for lunch. What a treat. We were not allowed to eat blackberries - I've no idea why - and when there was a Sister with us we never did but, with no Sister, we ate them with relish. This only happened when I was sixteen years old and was considered old enough to be in charge of the children. On these occasions I taught them how to drop a blackberry into the back of their throat and squash it so as to avoid detection.

Chapter 5

Sickness and Injury

... and when bleeding healed they wounds.
                    Cowper: Olney Hymns 18

With up to thirty of us cooped up together, sickness was common. So was injury, both mild and serious.

As a toddler I suffered from acute bronchitis, I had it quite often and according to Mouldy Cheese, I frightened everyone to death. She and Aggy Ragbag must have nursed me with great care for children as young as I was die very quickly from bronchitis; they must be looked after very closely and carefully. In the late '30s there were no antibiotics but to help them they would have had Dr Graham-Campbell. He was tall and gentle and he had a comforting, soothing voice, though I don't remember him from the bronchitis days. I don't remember the bronchitis. My first memory of Dr Graham-Campbell is associated with poisoning and even then it's vague.

Four of us were having a "tea party", in the garden and we had a lovely salad of sorrel, dandelion, clover and nasturtium leaves. We found some black, shiny seeds and added those as a special treat. I can still see the shiny black seeds on the paper we used as plates. I was sitting cross-legged with my back to the playroom - and that's about all I can remember. The black shiny seeds were from our laburnum tree and they are highly poisonous. Nausea and vomiting is followed by confusion, muscular inco-ordination, respiratory failure and death. Mustard comes to mind with vague recollections of Dr Graham-Campbell. I thought for a long time that we had been given mustard to make us sick but that is unlikely; more probably it would have been salt. Perhaps laburnum - or its effect - is hot. I remember that I couldn't be sick, I remember the bed I was in and the burning getting worse but who tried to induce the vomiting and with what is a total blank. All four of us survived, as far as I know. I was four years old.

I seem to have been very prone to injury at about that age. One day Mouldy Cheese sent me upstairs to find one of the Big Girls. Martha was up there and I told her that Mouldy Cheese wanted Sybil. Martha said that Sybil wasn't there but I insisted and threatened to "tell Sister". "Oh go away you little sneak". said Martha giving me a push. I fell backwards and I tumbled all the way downstairs screaming my head off and at some point I cut my chin. Mouldy Cheese rushed hotfoot to pick me up. There was blood everywhere and trouble all round. I accused Martha of pushing me though she could not have meant to push me downstairs. It was just that they were close behind me when she shoved me. Blood is a great dramatiser of any situation, however, and there was a lot of gefuffle. A piece of sticking plaster was stuck across the cut and I was put to bed. To this day I have a little scar on the point of my chin as a memento of that occasion.

In those days I slept in the same dormitory as a Big Girl called Sarah. It was her responsibility to put out the light once everyone was in bed. Apparently, I used to get out of bed and clutch at her leg while she was doing it and Sarah says it drove her mad. She was all of eleven years old. It made her really cross and one night she pushed me away as she switched off the light. I fell backwards and hit my head on an iron bedstead. I thought that warm water was running down my back but the water got sticky. It was blood. Sister came up and I was taken to the bathroom and my head put under the bath tap. The blood was washed away and sticking plaster applied. I was then given a clean nightie and put back to bed. No-one ever quite found out what had happened. I liked Sarah.

Then came Sister Thelma. I think we must have taken an instant and fierce dislike to each other. Sister Thelma could not stand me and I most emphatically hated and feared her. Perhaps it was my disabilities that Sister Thelma disliked so much. "The sins of the fathers..." and "orphan" equalled "sinner" in those days, in many people's eyes, especially to nuns. Many people can't cope with other people's disabilities anyway.

The treatment for hammer toes in the 1930s was to strap them firmly into their proper place. Under-over, under-over, the strapping brought the toes into line. My little toe was underneath its neighbours and the middle one touched the big toe underneath. It was the same on both feet. Having my toes brought into line like that was very uncomfortable, even painful if I was jumping about. I used to dread bath-time and it was a mercy that we only had one bath a week. I had to sit in the bath with both feet up on a very low stool, which was a great strain on my legs. When the strapping had to be changed, Mouldy Cheese and Aggy Ragbag were gentle. They would soak my feet in the bath, cut the strapping between the toes and ease it off but it was painful. Sister Thelma cut the strapping between the toes and ripped it off. There was no soaking first and it was agony.

My squint has always upset some people. At a distance it is not easy to see who I am looking at in a group. In my childhood, people would often ask: "What are you looking at?" and glance over their left shoulder. I would be looking at them so the question always seemed a strange one to me. Sister Thelma would say: "Look at me when I'm speaking to you," and she often slapped me hard. This always upset me because I had no idea what I had done wrong. Also, it was war-time when Sister Thelma took over and we had blue ceiling lights in all our rooms. Everyone else could see by them but they were useless to me. I might as well have been in the dark. I can see little or nothing in dim light and nothing at all in the dark. I was always bumping into things, falling over, or knocking things off tables. This infuriated Sister Thelma and she would tell me crossly to look where I was going or not to be so clumsy. I began to look on my "not seeing" and my clumsiness as a fault. After all, everyone else could see, even in the blue light.

Aggy Ragbag told me in a letter, about 40 years later when I asked her about those very early years: "... most of us loved you very much." The "most" clearly excluded Sister Thelma for she was merciless to me. When she punished me it certainly never hurt her more than it hurt me but it was much worse when I needed treatment.

The "Get up. You're not hurt." later turned us into stoics. Before that, when I needed treatment and Sister Thelma was "up" there was nothing stoical about me. I was a dissolving jellybaby. I would try to hide but that was useless. Sister Thelma would drag me to the place of torture, a disintegrating wimp.

The first time it happened I was rising six years old. I was run over by a bicycle and had nasty gravel rash on both legs. Sister Thelma scrubbed both legs hard with a nail-brush and it was agonising. I screamed and screamed but Sister Thelma had no ear drums. I struggled but it was like trying to get away from an octopus. The blood was washed away and dry lint and bandages applied. When Sister Thelma later ripped them off, she had to pin me down because both lint and bandage were firmly stuck.

When Sister Thelma had finished tending my legs she sent me back to school. Everyone at school was very kind and comforting and I revelled in the warmth. In the afternoon I was violently sick and taken back to the Orphanage. Sister Thelma sent me to bed and when Miss Russell came that afternoon I was not allowed to see her. Little girls who pretended to be ill did not deserve visitors, I was told. What a day. What a nightmare.

Had I always bitten my nails or did Sister Thelma start me off? I only remember the habit from her reign. I didn't just chew the ends; I tore the nails off down to the quick and this savagery often made them bleed. When I was really upset I chewed the skin off my knuckles as well so my hands were forever sore and looked a real mess. Sometimes I would be chewing hard and, out of nowhere, Sister Thelma would swipe my hand away from my mouth. "Don't chew your nails, you dirty little pig. You're disgusting." Sometimes I had a bit of nail or skin firmly grasped in my teeth and the swipe would tear the skin or nail and draw blood. Many remedies were tried but none worked. My nails were painted with bitter aloes but I went on chewing. My hands were tied to the edge of the bed at night but all this did was to give me a life-long dread of being restrained in any way.

I often had nightmares and one particular one came over and over again. I would be walking along and a Thing would be coming towards me. I thought it was kindly but it would suddenly turn into an enemy. I tried to run. I couldn't. Shoes solid and tight-fitting. I would try to drag my feet out of my shoes. I couldn't; the laces were gone. My shoes were stuck to the ground; the Thing coming faster, faster. Very near...Oh, God! I would wake up as the Thing was about to engulf me. I would try to sit up but I couldn't and with my hands tied to the bed my terror was magnified. It made the nightmare half-real. I never dared to cry out for help once I was awake, even though these were moments of stark, destroying fearfulness. All I had to soothe it was the cold, dark isolation of the dormitory.

Biting nails leads to septic fingers, called whitlows. Whenever I got a whitlow I tried to hide it but that was impossible. The big, fat, dark red finger was all too obvious. I couldn't use the hand for anything, anyway; the pain was too intense. I couldn't even eat with the hand affected. Inevitably, Sister Thelma would see the finger. "You disgusting child!" she would exclaim, "I'll have to deal with that horrible finger."

I know what it's like to wait for certain torture. The first time I didn't know so I went quietly to the bathroom with Sister Thelma. Never again. I struggled and fought every inch of the way. Sister Thelma would have a tin mug full of unbearably hot water ready - a sore finger can stand far less heat than a healthy one. Sister Thelma would hold me, clamped between her knees in her voluminous habit, with the rest of me pinioned across her knee by her bony elbow. The affected hand would be seized in a vice-like grip and the septic finger plunged into the water. It was held there until the pus had gathered then a needle would be sterilised with a match and stuck into the finger. The pus would burst out and an antiphlogisten poultice was applied. The deed was done. All through this torture I would try to pull away but Sister Thelma held me too tightly. The only thing I could do was to scream - and I screamed blue murder. One day Sister Thelma loosened her grip ever so slightly but it was enough. I twisted and sank my teeth into her arm. Sister Thelma cried out in pain and surprise; I had put everything I could into that bite. With incredible speed I was face down across her knees. Someone had left her hairbrush in the bathroom and Sister Thelma spanked me very hard and very long with it. Then the treatment continued to my tears but at least the water was less hot by that time. By contrast, Sister Monica, who came later, would dip the finger gently in and out of the water until it had cooled enough to hold the finger in all the time.

Sister Monica gave me the only glimpse of tenderness that I ever remember from my childhood. I was eight years old and I had measles. I had had my nightmare of The Thing and I woke in terror feeling desperately sick and ill. My fear of being sick on the floor far outweighed my fear of going to the lavatory so I got out of bed and started towards it. My hands were free that night. It was very difficult because I couldn't see where I was going and I had a long way to go. I had to cross our six-bedded dormitory, go across the end of the landing through another six-bedded dormitory and through the bathroom. Sister Monica's room was off the bathroom and I collapsed in a heap outside her door, holding on to the bath. Without really knowing how I got there I found myself lying on Sister Monica's bed.

Sister Monica took my temperature and said I would have to stay in bed; I had probably got measles. She was very gentle with me. She got my flannel and towel from the bathroom and washed my hands and face. As she came towards me with the flannel, I could smell a wonderful fragrance, like flowers in spring. I was entranced; it was the soap. Sister Monica washed my face and hands and the fragrance was on me. "Please don't wipe it off." I pleaded as she rinsed the flannel and brought it back. "Whyever not?" Sister Monica asked. She was amused. "It's lovely. Please leave it." I said. I had never smelt such scented soap before; it was Lifebuoy and Carbolic for us. "Don't worry. It stays a long time." Sister Monica said. She rinsed my hands and held one up to my nose. "Smell." She was right. The fragrance was still there and I went on sniffing my hand. Sister Monica wrapped me in a blanket, picked me up and started towards the door. In an instant I forgot about the perfume. I did not want to leave the gentleness and the friendly room; none of it existed outside. I put my head on Sister Monica's shoulder and began to cry. Sister Monica's gentleness immediately gave way to matter-of-fact Sister-firmness. "Whatever is the matter with you? she said bracingly. What are you crying for? You'll only

41

make yourself worse."

The dream was fading; the warmth was already going. I did not want to go back to the dormitory but Sister Monica took me back to my bed and tucked me in. "How do you feel now?" she asked, gentle again. I wanted to snuggle up to her; burrow into the warmth. I always felt like that if someone spoke kindly to me but I knew it was pointless. Sister Monica would get brusque and let's-be-sensible again. I turned my face to the wall. As time went by I curbed these feelings more and more; I was afraid of being pushed aside again. Soon I reached the point where I could not have responded to such moments even if I had dared.

Some illnesses, like scarlet fever or yellow jaundice, meant a spell in the Isolation Hospital and girls coming back from there said how wonderful it was. I tried so hard to get there when any of the others had an Isolation illness. We had an Isolation Room where a girl would be put while she was waiting for a transfer and I would sneak in there and sit on her bed, in the hope of catching whatever she had. No such luck. The only thing I didn't want was scabies; anyone with scabies was scrubbed with a brush and then painted. That sounded awful but scarlet fever or yellow jaundice would have been all right. It was a mercy that I got neither.

I had to wait till I was 12 years old to go to hospital. My hammer toes had not responded to being strapped up so they had to be straightened. I went to hospital with a girl from my class in school called Mavis. We were next to each other and her parents sat between our beds when they came. They used to bring things for me as well as for their daughter and so I never felt left out at visiting time. They were such thoughtful people. Having stitches and pins taken out of toes is not at all pleasant but I neither cried nor even moved. The nurses couldn't understand it but I had joined the stoics by then.

For six glorious weeks I was in hospital. Mavis, my friend, thought the food was horrid but I thought it was scrumptious. Towards the end of our stay there was a firework display for the wedding of Princess Elizabeth and Prince Philip and it was magnificent. Hospital was Wonderland. I did not want to go back to the Orphanage.

In the same year as I had measles I fell at school and cut my head on a stone wall. I was taken straight to Dr Graham-Campbell's surgery by one of our teachers. Dr Graham-Campbell said I needed two stitches and he sewed my head up without a local anaesthetic while I lay still and silent. As he bandaged my head he said: "What a brave girl you are, 'Topsy' " and he gave me a threepenny bit. It was not that I was brave. It was just that the "Get up. You're not hurt." training was fully in place by then. Afterwards, the teacher took me back to the Orphanage, holding my hand all the way. It was about 11 o'clock and Sister Thelma was "up". The teacher handed me over with explanations, and left. "What have you been doing?" asked Sister Thelma, "Fighting again, I suppose. Go to bed." I was pretty handy with my fists by that time so the accusation was not entirely misplaced.

I was still having accidents when I went to secondary school. For instance, when I was twelve years old, I fell over the ball one day when we were playing netball. The ball had dropped at my feet and I fell flat on my face over it, literally, my glasses smashing on the hard court. Luckily, no glass went into my eye - I was used to screwing my eyes up as I fell - but there were bits all around it. The games teacher picked up the remains of my glasses and I automatically expected to go on playing. "Don't be silly," she said, "You can't go on playing. We must see to that eye." She took me to the school treatment room and cleaned me up, putting a pad over the eye, and gave me a note for Sister Monica who had taken over from Sister Thelma by that time. "Now, be careful how you go." said the games mistress as she saw me off. I got much gentler treatment when I got back to the Orphanage. I was sent to bed but it did not feel like a punishment as it had always done with Sister Thelma. Sister Monica brought me some bread and milk - cubes of bread in hot milk, with sugar scattered over it - and checked that I was all right. We always had bread and milk at such times when Sister Monica was in charge. It was very soothing and easily eaten.

Two years later I developed sinusitis. Sister Monica had gone by then and Sisters Penelope and Annette were in place. The sinusitis was acute, very painful and most unpleasant. I had to go into hospital and I was given the new antibiotic - penicillin - by injection. When the nurse came to give me the first injection she said: "Turn over.

I'm going to give it to you in your bottom." No she was not! I had a corner bed and I scrabbled up into the corner, back to the wall, and refused to move. The nurse was very encouraging but I was adamant: "I won't have it." I kept saying. Eventually the nurse went away and came back with a doctor. He was firmer but I still refused to move. "I won't have it in my bottom." I insisted. I cannot imagine that they ever had any idea why but finally they decided to give it in my arms. Penicillin in the arm is very painful even for a well-covered person. I was match-stick thin and it was hell but I was not baring my behind to anyone.

I was not the only one who was afraid to bare her body; the rest of the girls were just the same though sometimes for different reasons. For example, one day a girl called Julie was out for a walk with the dogs. While they were off somewhere she took off her coat and amused herself by climbing up a hay-elevator or some such piece of machinery. At the top she nearly fell off so she threw her arm over the machinery to save herself. On some part of it, she cut herself under the armpit. It was not serious but it bled quite a lot. When Julie got back to the Orphanage she tried to keep her coat on because it was soaked with blood. Obviously, that was impractical and when Julie took off her coat the cut was revealed. "How did it happen?" Sister Penelope asked sternly. She dressed the wound and as she did so, Julie had to tell her how it had happened. "This time it isn't very bad." Sister Penelope said, wielding the strap. "Next time you might lose your arm. This is for being deceitful. Don't you ever do such a stupid thing again."

Chapter 6

Crime and Punishment

These children are dear to Me
Be a mother to them
And more than a mother
Watch over them tenderly.
Be just and kind.
If they weary thee
I will give thee strength.
If they are froward
I will be thy consolation
                    (Hung on the wall outside the parlour.)

We were brought up to believe that every thing we did, good or bad, was registered in a Book by the Recording Angel. On the Last Day everyone was judged by God according to whether the good outweighed the bad and sentence was passed appropriately.

We were also taught, explicitly and by implication, that we were wicked through and through. We were therefore in for a very bad time when we came up for Divine Trial. As a young child I always hoped, without much expectation, that my good deeds would help to cancel out the bad, especially as the Sisters already did a lot of God's work for Him. Many things we did or left undone were punishable, some more heinous than others. The seriousness of the crime and the severity of the sentence depended, basically, on two factors: the criminal law imposed by the two Sisters caring for us at any one period and whichever of the two was "up" when the offence was committed.

Some Sisters counteracted wrongdoing with physical

punishment; others with psychological retribution. Some, like Sister Eleanor, were incapable of doing either and we had shown how wrong *their* attitude was by running wild - hadn't we?

Until I was five years old the wages of sin were comparatively mild and their causes apparent. As I grew older the penalties became infinitely harsher and the reasons for them much more obscure. My earliest recollection of punishment is being slapped or given a short spanking for screaming whenever one of my phobias intruded on everyone's life. The kind of spanking I received for wetting the bed was a different kettle of fish. It was much harder, it was much longer, we were laid across the Sisters' knees and we were naked. Sometimes it was in public, which was mortifying; sometimes it was in private.

Whether the choice of public or private punishment was deliberate or not I was too young to know. The public ones may have been to make us ashamed of the particular sin we had committed, or it may just have depended on where we were at the time. Mouldy Cheese would have heard about the wet bed just before we went down to morning prayers so she might just have punished me there and then, which was why it was public.

The Devil is supposed to find work for idle hands to do. If so, I must say that he was a great help in keeping me occupied. When I was three and a half years old I was put behind the laundry door for chattering too much in the dormitory. I was probably already very tired so I climbed into a big, round ironing basket on a low shelf behind the door, wrapped myself in the ironing blanket and sheet and went to sleep. The Sisters went frantic trying to find me, according to Mouldy Cheese who told me of it.

As I grew older I found other things to fill in the time behind the door, like swinging on the roller towel. There was one behind both the laundry and the lobby door. For a little girl, the fold in the roller towel was just the right height for slipping the arms in and swinging from side to side. One day I was a bit too enthusiastic in my swinging and the towel was an old one. It tore, with a loud and sickening noise and down came the towel, roller and all. The roller clanked on the stone floor and the kitchen was within earshot. I got the inevitable up-ending and my sentence was extended.

When I was five years old Sister Thelma took over from Mouldy

Cheese and Aggy Ragbag. I can't remember who the second one was with Sister Thelma; Sister Thelma lowered too heavily over my world. She was tall, thin, mean and menacing and much more than a stern disciplinarian. The fear I had had of her at the start increased as time passed.

Sister Thelma was certainly one of those who believed that orphans were sinners by nature. The harsher the treatment was the more thoroughly would our sins be wiped out and Sister Thelma was no slacker. For her, the cause of sin wasn't important. She only recognised its effects and she punished them severely. Two episodes are imprinted for ever on my memory. Often, the prelude to retribution was a Summons to the parlour. Outside the door were God's words of encouragement to the Sisters at the beginning of this chapter. They are engraved on my mind for ever. "Joan, (as my name was then) Sister wants you in the parlour." was enough to turn my blood to water, especially when the Summons came from Sister Thelma. Being Sent For could be anything from chastisement to parents coming to fetch us home. For me, with Sister Thelma, I knew that it always meant trouble, usually with a capital C. Sister Thelma never spanked us; she was much handier with the bamboo cane.

We children developed a philosophy about punishment very early in life. If we deserved it for committing a recognised crime and the punishment was fair, we took it with as much fortitude as possible. If it was unjust, we were resentful and our mistrust increased.

The first episode with Sister Thelma happened when I was about seven years old. I used to get very bored with church services and one Sunday, to relieve the tedium, I was jostling my neighbour when I should have been praying. She fell off her hassock and Sister Thelma, behind us, had seen all. A long, bony finger prodded me in the back and I had the rest of the service to think about the consequences. Back at the Orphanage it was into the parlour for me. Sister Thelma took out the cane and I stared at it nervously during the build-up: "You are a naughty, wicked girl. If you don't mend your ways you will go to the Lake which burns with fire and brimstone." I never did know what brimstone was but that was unnecessary; The Lake of Fire, the Devil and Hell were quite enough to scare me out of my wits. "You must be punished for misbehaving in God's House. God is not mocked. Shall I cane you or send you to bed?" No contest. Caning was very painful but soon over whereas being sent to bed, usually without any food for the rest of the day, was dreadful eternity. I chose the cane. I stuck out my hand and shut my eyes. A whistling thwack cut across the fingers of each hand, making them unusable for some time afterwards. Shutting my eyes stopped me from pulling my hand away; that would have been very unwise. Caning over, I turned towards the door, trying not to cry and squeezing my hands under my armpits. "Now go to bed." came the icy command. I couldn't believe my ears. I had made my choice, taken my punishment and that should have been that. The tears spilled over. This was unfair. "Perhaps that will help you to mend your ways, you little heathen. I'm tired of your frowardness." I didn't know what "frowardness" was either when I was small; only that it was very bad and always involved unpleasant consequences. Sister Thelma went on in the same vein but I was hardly listening. I was absorbing the fact that grown-ups were not to be trusted.

The second episode happened when I was ten years old. It was near the end of World War II and Mabel, our evacuee, was about to go home. Mabel and I were friends and we were on the playroom table - a big wooden one with benches on either side. Mabel was lying on her back and I was sitting beside her. We were talking about Mabel's going home and Mabel, having no idea what she was saying murmured: "I don't expect you'll ever go home, will you?" Poor Mabel. She was only being kind but its effect was startling. I was already eight and a half years on the way to nowhere, totally abandoned by my parents, and the pent-up feelings, frustrations, miseries and unhappiness burst out. I banged my bunched-up fist down on to her nose. All Hell broke loose. Mabel began shrieking, blood was all over the place and Sister Thelma arrived at the double. We were both taken to the laundry and, while Mabel explained incoherently what had happened, I tried to tell Sister Thelma that it wasn't all my fault. She was not impressed. Anyway, I couldn't really explain why I had lost control; it was much too personal. Mabel was cleaned up and sent somewhere to recover, while I was beaten and put behind the lobby door. "to reflect on your sins, you little savage."

I did not reflect on my sins. I thought about not having a mother and father like Mabel to come and take me home. I thought about never having seen or heard from them. I thought about how terrifying Sister Thelma was and I cried and cried into the roller towel.

When I was eight years old Sister Monica came from Chapter Meeting to join Sister Thelma. Sister Monica was one of those who never used physical measures, though she knew well enough how to control us. She used God as a weapon. The only physical method she used was to slap us quite hard on both cheeks if we dared to interrupt one of her Holy Lectures. "What do you think you are entitled to? Who rescued you from the gutter and brought you to where you are today? God. You are nurtured through the charity of others and don't you forget it." God, in His Immeasurable Goodness and Boundless Mercy, had provided us with everything. At the end of three or four years of this, I knew that, whatever God had provided us with, we were not dear to Him. We were undeserving, worthless, often ungrateful; garbage from the gutter, rubble on the heap. God did not like little girls like us.

Sister Monica also favoured sending us to bed and withholding Sunday sweets. Being sent to bed was an awful penance. It could be for hours if the sentence started early in the day, as it had with the church episode. We also had nothing to eat for the rest of the day - The Fast of Repentance, I suppose. By the time I was seven years old I had thought up several games to while away the time, my favourite being to play with postage stamps. I used to take all the stamps I could find out of the rubbish box because I liked the colours - red, green, blue, brown, orange - and hide them away. One day when I was in bed in disgrace I thought how nice it would be if I could play with my stamps. Later on I took them upstairs ready for next time and hid them in a huge chest of drawers in our dormitory, underneath some stuff which wasn't used very often. Thereafter, when I was sent to bed I would get out my stamps and play.

There were dozens of combinations for dividing the stamps: colour, monarch, colour and monarch, value and so on. I used to play sitting cross-legged half-way down the bed, with the bed-clothes turned back. Then, if anyone came to check on me, I could lie down and whip the bed-clothes over the stamps in no time. The groupings would be Big Girls/Little Girls/Sisters and so on. Any new stamp would be a new girl. She would be one of three kinds; she might get angry, or be silent or cry all the time, like new girls always did. Whichever sort the "new girl" was, she wouldn't be accepted for a while. New girls were very boring for me at that age because they never wanted to play at first. Often they would have sisters and they would stay together and weep. So in my game, the "new girl" would be kept aside when she was first introduced to the group. She would be allotted a Big Girl, who would tell her to "shut up" if she cried and she would be punished a lot because she didn't know how to behave; my Orphanage version of Mums and Dads. Apart from the hunger of the Penitential Fast, playing with the stamps made being sent to bed much more fun.

Witholding Sunday sweets might follow a minor sin or it might be added to sterner measures. After lunch on Sundays little piles of sweets - 3, 4 or 5 - were put on a large tray and each girl took her pile under close supervision. The tray was never over-crowded because several children would have incurred the "no sweets" penalty during the week. This was not a wholly effective punishment because a girl with sweets would secretly give her friend one when no-one was looking. These donations had to be eaten with great discretion because a girl who was out of favour might "split", hoping to get back in favour. Sometimes the "split-on" would get what was coming to her; sometimes the "splitter" for telling tales. "Splitting" was therefore a dicey business.

A really dreadful punishment was being sent down into the cellar. I would rather have had a really merciless beating than go down there. There was a small, grimy window at the top of one wall, on a level with the pavement outside but it gave very little light. The cellar did have a low wattage electric light but we were not allowed to have it on when we were down there in disgrace. I could see almost nothing and I used to creep down there in fear and trembling, knowing that cockroaches and spiders awaited me. It was never quite so bad after Harvest Festival because we always got several large marrows and, sick-making though they might be to eat, they were very good for getting off the ground. Cockroaches couldn't, or didn't, climb up the sides - though spiders could - and by sitting cross-legged on a marrow we could prevent cockroaches from running over our feet. Nothing stopped the spiders from crawling over us though and to feel one tip-tip-toeing over my skin would drive me into a frenzy. I would knock it off, if I could reach it, and brush frantically at my skin long after the spider had gone.

When the change-over of Sisters came in my 13th year, things went from bad to worse. Sister Penelope had replaced Sister Monica and Sister Annette came back to replace Sister Eleanor. Sister Annette's reappearance brought the rioting to an end and we settled down to a new and much harsher regime. Punishment became more terrible and much more unpredictable. The bamboo cane gave place to a leather strap and, as we acquired three dogs, the strap gave way to a cat o'four tails - two doubled up dogs' leashes. Thrashings carried out by Sister Penelope with the cat o'four tails were merciless and never private. Even when conducted on a one-to-one basis, the sufferer's screams could be heard far and wide. If any of us were near the laundry or the backhouse, where whippings took place, we could also hear the menacing *hhwtt* of the cat o'four tails through the air. It used to turn my stomach. It was even worse if we had to hold one of the little ones down and I used to get out of the way if it seemed likely. Having to do that used to make me feel ill.

One girl, Polly, who wet the bed almost every night, was whipped, naked, the following morning, and wrapped in her wet sheets. I met this girl years later and she made two comments about her time in the Orphanage: "It were a wonder no-one ever stuck a knife in 'er (Sister P's) back". and: "I either 'ad me face on the mangle or me 'ead in the cellar." That about summed up life for poor Polly.

When two girls were whipped so hard that their thighs bled, I'd had enough and I secretly wrote to the Inspector and asked for help. Quite why I don't know, but I thought Inspector B was a policeman so I sent the letter to the police station. The letter reached him all right but I needn't have bothered. The Inspector told the Reverend Mother that he was coming and the Reverend Mother told Sister Penelope. I was whipped for my malice and deception by Sister

Penelope and torn to pieces by the Reverend Mother for my wickedness and ingratitude. I was dared to try it again. No fear. There was no forcing a gap in the solidarity of Authority. They were all in league with each other and we didn't stand a chance.

Sister Penelope had a very short and violent temper. Her anger could flash from nowhere and heaven help the girl who had caused it if she were within reach. She would be clouted with anything to hand or kicked if she had her back to Sister Penelope.

I was in the kitchen one day when Sister Penelope lost her temper with me. I had sworn at her and she got really angry. I had trodden on my rabbit's front paw because I couldn't see the animal against the asphalt in the yard and I was very upset about it. The rabbit had screamed and Sister Penelope had called me a clumsy fool. "I didn't mean to hurt the bloody rabbit." I answered back, angry in my turn, and turned towards the door. Out of the blue, Sister Penelope kicked me really hard between the legs. The pain was so intense that it stopped me breathing and the kick knocked me off my feet. Outside the kitchen door was a square of red tiles, which linked the kitchen with the lobby across the end of the hall. There was a wall along one side running at right angles to the kitchen. I can still see those red tiles coming up to meet me as I fought for breath. Almost as soon as I hit the floor I rolled over with my back against the wall and curled up into a ball of agony and defence. I had made the mistake of turning my back on Sister Penelope. I never made it again.

We were all pretty good at ducking away from blows. Since I could always see much better in my right eye than in the left I always ducked to the right. I didn't often escape completely and my left shoulder often took the blow from a rolling pin, an old-fashioned heavy pop bottle, the copper stick or anything else to hand. I now have very painful arthritis in that shoulder. Our heads often received the benison of saucepan, plate, wooden spoon or book, which made us see stars. Such a blow was usually too sudden and too unexpected for us to put our hands over our heads or duck away.

Sister Annette, on the other hand, used her razor-like tongue. She often denigrated us or set the other children against us - like when they wouldn't hold my hands in circle games. She was also cruel in other ways, as when she made Polly sweep up the leaves in the yard *against* the wind. Polly was on a hiding to nothing and would be outside on a cold, late Autumn day, uselessly sweeping at the leaves. Sister Annette taught us to call Polly "Dippy", - which, in Wiltshire, means soft in the head - because she was a slow learner. Sister Annette also said that Polly would contaminate the rest of us so she wasn't allowed to play with us. Instead, she had to sit in the backhouse making dusters - the equivalent of picking oakum. Sometimes a punishment would be purely capricious. For example, we were going on holiday one year and a girl called Katie asked Sister Annette, as a joke, if we were taking the mangle with us. Sister Annette wasn't in a laughing mood so she told Sister Penelope and the joke was on Katie. Sister Penelope said that if Katie was that fond of the mangle she could say goodbye to it. Face down on the mangle, Katie learned that jokes were likely to backfire.

Quite the most bizarre and the most fearsome punishment was being sent into the garden to face the bantam cock. To see this happen stoked up the fires of anger and guilt within me; anger because of what these so-called Sisters of Mercy did to little children; guilt because I hadn't got the guts to say "Don't." I watched, or heard, several children suffer this dreadful penalty and it made me sick with fear. I shared the little girl's suffering and terror because I knew what the cockerel was like. He was presumably guarding his harem of hens but his peck and his ferocious flying attack were murderous. Whenever I hung out the washing I would cover Cocky with a sheet; then I would snatch the sheet off and drop the large laundry basked over him. Finally, I would grab the basket and bolt for the house, using the basket as a shield, always desperately afraid that Cocky would get past it - and I was a teenager. Only when a little girl nearly had her eye pecked out did I speak. "Please," I urged Sister Penelope, "bring her in. He'll have her eye out." Sister Penelope had paused in her pastry-making to watch the fun. The rolling pin crunched down on to my left shoulder before I had time to dodge. "You mind your own business, Joan Hall" roared Sister Penelope, "You're too cheeky by half." but she brought the child in. That was the second and last time I ever intervened.

From time to time we would dare answer back or even fight back-like Jessica with the shoes. Mostly we just ducked or covered up and hoped it wouldn't hurt too much. The commonest way of "breaking out", however, was to Run Away. Girls had been Running Away ever since I had been at the Orphanage but they always had to come back. There was nowhere else to go. They were punished for their trouble but at least they had let off steam. Polly often Ran Away, sometimes even going to the police station. That was when she was sorely afraid and hoped that the police would help. It wasn't obvious that the police did anything but perhaps Polly was saved a few beatings because the police always brought her back.

All this had and has lasting repercussions. For instance, I often ducked whenever someone raised a hand too quickly and I wouldn't turn my back even when, after leaving the Home, it was safe. It was decades before I could undress without feeling threatened and it had nothing to do with prudishness. One effect is permanent. I can't hear the sound of an angler casting his line without cringing inside. It sounds just like the noise of a whip-lash and it still makes me feel uneasy. If I'm not expecting it, it turns my stomach just like it used to. We hear it often, living by the Kennet and Avon canal and when there are too many anglers, I have to go somewhere where I can't hear it. Several anglers casting together make it sound too much like a thrashing. All that is missing are the screams.

Chapter 7

God and the Devil

Christ is the Head of This House;
The Unseen Guest at Every Meal;
The Silent Listener to Every Conversation.
>   (Text hanging in the hall of the Orphanage)

Terrorist: one who favours or uses terror-inspiring methods of Government or of coercing Government or community.
>   (Oxford English Dictionary)

The Convent from which we were ruled was very High Anglican. Every morning, before breakfast, we prayed in our little chapel. Whenever we used the name of Jesus, even in ordinary conversation, we had to half-genuflect.

> *At the name of Jesus*
> *Every knee shall bow ...*
>   (Hymns: Ancient and Modern)

In chapel we would say prayers, then sing a hymn:

> *Jesus loves me this I know,*
> *For the Bible tells me so;*
> *Little ones to Him belong;*
> *they are weak but He is strong...*
> *Gentle Jesus, meek and mild,*
> *Look upon a little child...*

The chapel was spick and span, as befitted the House of God and the altar was dressed in the appropriate colour. At times of major Christian Festivals we used to go to the Convent for Vespers at six o'clock in the evening. For Vespers we had to wear pale blue veils over our heads and our hair was totally covered, like the Sisters'. In our veils we had to walk down the road to the Convent and we prayed that none of our schoolmates would be about. If they were they used to mock us all the way there. The Convent chapel was always full of candles and incense and I loved the brightness and the smell. As we went in we genuflected to the Cross standing free in the Chancel - a huge one to my child's eye.

On the day of our patronal festival we used to go to tea at the Convent before Vespers. By everyone's plate there was always a delicate little arrangement of Autumn leaves and flowers; a Virginia creeper leaf, with a sprig of spindle and a Michaelmas daisy arranged on it. They were beautiful and with one at about 120 places at the tables the effect was breathtaking. I don't remember the actual tea; only those captivating little posies and the beauty of the dining room.

We spent a lot of time in church and I grew to hate Sundays. Early Communion or, alternatively, Sung Eucharist, 11 o'clock Matins and Evensong. The only good thing I recall about church was the golden light streaming through the west window during Evensong at the right time of year. In a strange way it used to comfort me, even as a little girl - The Peace of God which passeth all understanding. Apart from that magnificent light I knew little of that Peace.

We were confirmed at a fairly early age and that was when Holy Communion was added to my Sunday misery. I used to faint quite often at Early Communion and Sisters Penelope and Annette would have gone on believing that it was attention-seeking if it had not been for a stand-in Sister. Sister Annette was on holiday and one Sunday Sister Elizabeth remarked to Sister Penelope after Sung Eucharist how very pale I looked and added: "Perhaps we should ask the Bishop for a dispensation?" I heard this but I had no idea what a "dispensation" was. It was granted in due course by the Bishop of the Diocese and turned out to be a cup of hot, sweet tea out of the Sister's early morning pot, which I had before going to

Communion. Only one Sister came to the early service with us. The other one went to Sung Eucharist later with a few of the older girls. She it was who had her early tea. I never fainted again in church. I sometimes faint now, though, if I have to "get up and go" before I have had anything to eat or drink in the morning.

Harvest Festival service always had a particular interest for us because we knew that most of the offerings to God would be passed on to us, especially the flowers. The church always had the earthy, Autumnal scent of dahlias and Michaelmas daisies, of fruit and vegetables. I used to pray that there would be no marrows but there were always dozens.

The service I hated most was the Collection Day Service for the orphans. Four of us would be chosen to make the collection while a suitable hymn was sung:

> *We are but little children weak,*
> *Nor born in any high estate;*

I was chosen when I was four years old and I did it for three years. We went up to the Chancel to receive our Collection bags - cloth bags, gathered on to a wooden ring at the top, with a wooden handle either side. Those bags could hold quite a lot of money. "Poor little things!" people would murmur as they stuffed their pounds, shillings and pence into the bags. I loathed it.

The Orphanage was voluntary and always short of money so these services were necessary but I hated having to be a Collector of Alms. It has left me with a lifelong diffidence about collecting. I always have, and still loathe doing it, though I can smother my dislike of it if the cause is good enough. I never mind selling something but just asking for money embarrasses me.

Good Friday was the last straw; the Stations of the Cross at 10 a.m. and the Three Hour Service from 12 mid day - 3 p.m. - all on an empty stomach. We observed the Fast from waking until we got back to the Orphanage after 3 o'clock but at least I was allowed my cup of tea. We also had to observe the Greater Silence so we weren't allowed to talk either. As I sat through sermon after sermon and sang hymn after dreary hymn, I used to wish heartily that Jesus Christ hadn't taken so long to die.

The one bright light in that awful Three Hours was the hymn: "O Sacred Head surrounded / By Crown of piercing thorns...". When sung really well, the harmonies in that hymn are very beautiful and very moving. As year followed year the words began to lose their meaning but the music stirs me even now. It would be one of my Desert Island discs. For services such as the Three Hour and Sung Eucharist on Sundays and Festivals, the students from the nearby Theological College used to come to church. They augmented the choir and the deep, rich sound of their singing was divine.

As time went by I found religion and its expression in church more and more difficult to reconcile with everyday life. We were reminded over and over again about God's Boundless Mercy; about being brought up on Charity "and don't you forget it." As if we could. God cared for everyone, we were told, down to the tiniest creature. He noticed even when a sparrow fell. Lucky sparrows. He didn't seem to notice or care much about what happened to us.

> *... our dear Lord was crucified*
> *And died to save us all.*

Not for us he didn't. When we were naughty we were threatened with God's wrath and retribution and with Hell and Damnation.

I had once committed such a wicked sin that my already growing fear of God was turned to terror by Sister Thelma. It was when I had measles, along with six of the other girls. We were convalescing and one day, bored with being cooped up, I looked for something to relieve the tedium. I found it; my blanket had its stitching left on it at one end. Half-afraid, half-excited, I pulled at the woollen thread and a little bit came undone. Soon, with the help of the other girls, the whole lot was unravelled.

We children knew where all the red lights were but sometimes we went straight through them. We could convert innocent fun into disaster in a few seconds and the results could be catastrophic.

We found a few more edges to unstitch and made the little heap of wool we had accumulated into a ball. With the excitement that mounting danger brings we began to play "catch". Our throws to each other got wilder and wilder and suddenly I fell out of bed. Aghast, we all lay down and pretended to be reading - and waited for Nemesis. It came all too soon. Our dormitory was over the parlour, Sister Thelma was "up" and she was in the parlour at that precise moment. She came charging upstairs and into our dormitory. "Whatever are you children doing? What happened?" Sister Thelma had fixed a girl called Daisy with her gimlet eyes. Daisy had no choice. She paused but she had to tell. "We were playing ball, Sister. Joan fell out of bed." Sister Thelma skewered me with a cold, steely stare and asked "What with?" I tried a lie. I often did to avoid the sterner penalties but it never worked; the lie was always writ large on my face. My friend of the moment tried to give me support behind Sister Thelma's back, by poking out her tongue. I giggled in fear and Sister Thelma was incensed. "It's no laughing matter, Miss. I'm waiting." I slowly, slowly pulled the huge ball from under the bed-clothes. It was one inch in diameter. Uselessly I clutched at the bed-clothes but Sister Thelma's grip matched her eyes; hard and cruel. The crinkled edge of blanket was revealed. I knew what to expect and my muscles began to twitch but this time I was quite wrong. Sister Thelma tore me into little tiny pieces and offered me up to God as a sacrifice: "You are a very wicked girl. You are deceitful and you tell lies and you are a bad influence on the other girls. All liars shall have their part in the Lake which burns with fire and brimstone. God doesn't like little girls like you. You had better say your prayers very carefully and hope that He will forgive you. He watches everything you do and listens to everything you say. He is everywhere and you can't escape Him. I shan't punish you. God Himself punishes children as wicked as you." Engraved on my memory for ever, those words filled me with annihilating terror. Sister Thelma stalked out and I buried myself under the bed-clothes. I prayed, I pleaded with God to forgive me, just this once, but He wasn't listening. That night I called the BOBS. I needed their help and comfort so badly but they weren't able to give either.

With the hostility and fear which had grown in me since Sister Thelma's arrival, I had invented the BOBS soon after she came. They were square or round, rather like robots but they could think. In moments of crisis they would completely surround my bed and I could sleep safely; no-one could get at me with the BOBS there. Usually I could only summon them at night, though. Even though it was daytime, I called to them in this desperate hour of need but they could offer nothing. On that dreadful day God strode out of church and towered over me in my daily life. He was accompanied by the Devil and, between them, they both soon played havoc with whatever peace of mind I had had.

The devil lurked in every corner laying traps for me and God grabbed me by the scruff of the neck whenever I got caught in them. It was very unfair. They could see me but they were invisible and I was scared witless by their cat-and-mouse games. I had become aware of God's inhumanity to Man. I was confused, bewildered, terrified and angered by God. If Jesus Christ had had anything to offer, God had completely overruled Him. It was really God who was Head of This House.

The hymns we sang and prayers we muttered in church and chapel were all frauds;

> *Alleluia not as orphans*
> *Are we left in sorrow now.*

We were orphans all right and there wasn't much we didn't know about sorrow.

> *To Mercy, Pity, Peace and Love*
> *All pray in their distress ...*

Sister Thelma had made it quite clear that we weren't entitled to any of that. Although she commanded us to pray, it was pointless. God never listened to us.

> *Lighten our darkness, we beseech Thee, O Lord.*

He never did. He only made it worse. I grew more and more angry with God. It was obvious that he was on the Sisters' side. I didn't know the word then but I saw Him as a terrorist. He coerced the Government in the Orphanage to terrorise us and the Sisters did

His bidding. Whenever I heard the *hhwt hhwt* I wanted to cry out loud: "Where are you, God? Are you listening? Don't you care?" I wanted to accuse the Sisters:

> "Inasmuch as ye have done it unto
> one of the least of these my brethren,
> ye have done it unto Me:"

What was the point? It was God's idea in the first place. His Wrath would have seen to it that I was next in line for the cat-o'-four-tails. Anyway, I was too much of a coward. I had tried twice; the plea for help to the Inspector and the appeal to Sister Penelope to bring the little girl, Janet, in from the bantam cockerel. Both episodes had had their very painful sequels.

Once we were confirmed we had to make our Confession once a month. We had to copy sins out of a little Black Book and read the list to the Chaplain of the Convent. I used to wonder if the Sisters made a full Confession and whether they had their own little Black Book:

> I have mercilessly whipped little children.
> I have been cruel.
> I don't care about the gutter-snipes.

"Guttersnipe" was an epithet we lived with all the time. I sometimes wondered if the Sisters made their Confessions at all. One Holy Saturday (the day before Easter Day) this wondering made me dangerously angry. A visiting Merthyr Brother had taken the Three Hour Service and he had talked about wisdom and kindliness in a way which had made me listen. I was old enough by that time to choose to go to him to make my Easter Confession and I did. "... I have sinned in the following ways," - I didn't bother with the Black Book any more - "and I ask of you, Father, counsel, penance and absolution."

After my Confession Brother Bernard really did give me counsel and absolution. I felt somehow cleansed. I was first in the queue so was in and out quite quickly.

I got back to the Orphanage before Sister Annette expected me. She was "up", unfortunately for us both. "You've been mighty quick." she said suspiciously. I told her I was the first in; that was why I had been so quick. Sister Annette didn't believe me and said so. My anger, never far below the surface, erupted. "I don't care what the hell you believe," I retorted, "my Confession is a matter between God and myself and none of your damn business." Thus I committed several sins in one sentence and washed away all the Sanctifying Grace I had just received from making Confession. I was sorely tempted to ask Sister Annette how she ever dared to make hers. Was there no end to it?

One evening, in my seventeenth year, I stood up to say the Creed. I was still at the Orphanage because I was still at school.

"I believe in God the Father Almighty,"

I paused. A hammer-blow hit my mind. Did I?

"And in His Son, Jesus Christ..."

No. Jesus Christ couldn't do anything without His Father's permission. There is no Father and no Son and no Devil. I wanted to shout it to the vaulting of the roof. A fifteen-year reign of confusion and terror came to an abrupt end. What a relief. What a release. The golden light streamed through the west window. It brought great peace to my sorely troubled and battered soul.

> There was Good and there was Evil.
> Sisters like Thelma and Annette were evil.
> Sisters like Eleanor were good.
> Sisters like Penelope were a mixture.

I could mouth the rest of the service so that there was no trouble from the Sisters. The service itself meant nothing to me now so it didn't matter. I was shot of God and the Devil and their terrorisation for ever. I didn't tell anyone; it was my carefully guarded and deeply hidden secret. I went to church and made the right noises but

Confession was too difficult to dodge in the Orphanage; it would have been too risky to let my secret out. Anyway, I was at boarding school by that time so I only had to make Confession about four times in a year during the holidays at the Orphanage. I could sometimes get away with it even then by electing to go to a visiting priest at the church and I then just sat in a pew at the back for a while. Sometimes, though, I was sent to our own chaplain at the Convent where all the other girls always went. No escape then but I could stomach it twice a year even though I found it difficult. Mouthing a service was one thing; no-one else was involved and I could miss out the bits I really couldn't say. Making Confession was quite another because then I was suborning a priest to give me counsel and absolution when the whole thing was a sham. I was heartily glad when I never had to do it again.

Chapter 8

Missing People

*Can a woman's tender care
Cease towards the child she bear?*
                              Cowper: Olney Hymns, 18.

I was at the Orphanage for seventeen and a half years and I was its
longest-serving inmate ever. Actually, in 1948 the Children's Act
of that year decreed that we no longer lived in Orphanages; we lived
in Children's Homes and we were no longer orphans; we were
deprived children. Our name was duly changed to The Haven,
though we girls weren't bowled over by it. At the time when we
became deprived children living at The Haven, the treatment of us
was going from bad to worse.

During my time I watched so many girls come and go and I saw
so many changes. We never did have many babies but as the years
went by we had almost none. Also, as the bigger girls who came
stayed at The Haven for a much shorter time so the population
became a much more shifting one. Not many girls were "single"
like me. Most had one, two or even three sisters with them and I
often wonder now if that helped at all. Some children had family
visitors and letters and cards. All letters in and out were censored
so they always felt tarnished to me. Not that there was much to
tarnish. Until my teens I had very few. Miss Russell used to send
Christmas, Easter, birthday and annual holiday cards but she was
the only one. She also came to see me once or twice a year and I
used to look forward to those visits, my only ones. I can still
remember her light grey car standing outside the Orphanage. I told
her this when I met her in the 1980's and she was astonished. "I got

rid of that in 1939, before the war." she said. I was then four years old. I don't remember much about her visits except the car. Many children had more visits than I did but I didn't envy them. Often those children got empty promises, many times repeated: " I'll be coming to take you home soon." Better no visit than that.

I had brought the BOBS into being as my supporters against the hostility and fear in my life but they were also my companions in the emptiness of my world. Not only did they come to me almost every night to sort out anyone who had ill-treated me; they also made a special point of coming when any of the other girls had had a visitor. They were very faithful and they were totally trustworthy and we had some very happy times together.

I don't think there were many friendships amongst us children at the Orphanage. I remember easily who were sisters but I couldn't say who were friends together. The shifting population meant that friendships were kaleidoscopic anyway; even at the age when friendships are more permanent. I certainly didn't make any friends in the Orphanage; I couldn't because I didn't know how. It wasn't very easy for me, anyway, because I was outside the run of normal Orphanage life for a lot of the time. I only saw the other girls at weekends and during the holidays when I was at Grammar School. Later, when I had to go to a special boarding school because of my poor sight, I only saw them in the holidays. We children didn't talk to each other much about anything that mattered. For example, when I went to boarding school, the other girls had no idea where I had gone. I heard later that they thought I had gone home and they were all very surprised when I reappeared at Christmas.

With the changing pattern, girls left quite often. The older ones left school when they were fourteen - or, from 1947, fifteen - and went to various jobs; younger ones went home or were adopted; new ones came. There were three types of new girl. Angry ones who made a lot of noise, banged furniture, beat walls, screamed and generally caused mayhem. They were suppressed by whatever retributive system was in operation at the time. Then there were the quiet ones, who were timid and unsociable at the beginning. They soon settled down and joined us on the heap of rubble. The third type was hard to handle. We couldn't get to know them at all. Often there were two or three sisters together and they cried together. "Mummy, I want my mummy," the little one would wail and her older sister(s), crying too, would try to comfort her. If the little one were on her own it was even worse. She would cry quietly in a corner, continuously and alone. Every now and then she would call with a choked wail: "Mummy! Where's my mummy?" As a little girl, that kind of crying upset me but I soon learned not to cry too. When I was older it tore me to pieces. It stirred my own dormant misery and left me feeling forsaken and alone.

We girls didn't talk to each other about these things either. We all had the same secrets; there were missing people in all our lives. I never knew how the others felt but I could guess. Sometimes I could hardly bear the pain and I would deliberately provoke one of the Sisters to relieve some of the torment. To provoke Sister Penelope was asking for trouble. With her short-temper she was easily roused and she was like a charging rhinoceros. To provoke Sister Annette was to irritate a spitting cobra. Sister Eleanor was unprovokable; just desperately hurt. With such pain inside I needed anger and violence to assuage it.

I found this out one day quite by chance when I was thirteen years old. Carol, a new little girl, was sobbing listlessly, all by herself in the cloakroom. I had been sent to fetch someone from the playroom and I could hear Carol as I went by. Suffering with her, I went back to the kitchen. "Where's Susan?" asked Sister Penelope crossly, "Why isn't she with you?" "She's coming." I answered shortly, immersed in my own hell. A rolling pin crashed down on to my shoulder. Inward-looking, I hadn't seen it coming so I didn't duck. "Don't be so insolent, Joan Hall." roared Sister Penelope, like an angry lion. My misery turned to anger. "You're a great big bully," I shouted, tears of pain running down my cheeks. Wham! The rolling pin came down again. This time I dodged and the rolling pin glanced off the same shoulder. The agony was such that it focussed all my attention on my shoulder and absorbed some of my inner hurt. I backed out of the kitchen and went into the laundry to hide my tears from everyone.

About three years later it wasn't Sister Penelope I provoked. Lisa was a little girl who cried forlornly all the time: "When am I going home? When is my mummy coming?" They weren't questions we could answer and the cries probed my own despair. We knew Lisa would probably never go home anyway. One Saturday, when Lisa's mother brought her back from an outing, she started: "I'll soon come and take you home. Just a bit longer." I was in the backhouse and Lisa and her mother were going through to the playroom. I was suddenly tired of it all. I couldn't bear it any longer and I lost my temper. "You lying, deceitful bitch. Why the bloody hell don't you take her home or stop making promises you're not going to keep..." I went on and on until I ran out of things to say.

I stomped off before Lisa's mother had regained her wits. She hadn't had time to say a word; she just stood with her mouth open. Lisa was already crying miserably when she came into the backhouse. By the time I charged away she was sobbing noisily in sheer fright. I was so angry with Lisa's mother that I couldn't have stopped my fury fizzing out even if I'd wanted to. I was angry hearing the same old promises, which I knew would never be kept; I was angry that children were left to cry in desolation - a desolation which echoed and tapped my own deeply buried feelings. At least my mother didn't come making false promises ... she just didn't come. I was very lucky that Sister Annette was upstairs at the time. I was even luckier that Sister Penelope was "down". If she had heard about it she would have flayed me alive.

These outbursts were few and far between and usually private but they got more and more violent. The other girls knew very little about them and thought I was very quiet. Since there was no love or care in the Orphanage I spent a lot of time looking for some and seeking attention. Not in the Orphanage, of course; the less attention I got there the better. I was looking all the time for someone special.

Someone who would say: "Well done." "Very good." "What a lovely picture." -anything to show that I had done something good and that someone cared that I had but the more I sought praise the less I got. It was clear that the Sisters were right. I was worthless and, certain of this, if anyone did praise me I was sure that they didn't mean it. I couldn't believe that it was true. I became self-centred and I grew up with the idea that if anyone was cross or angry in my presence it was my fault. I needed people to be pleased with me; if they weren't I tried harder to make them so. It was a very vicious circle. In the Orphanage we were constantly criticised and castigated and I was forever being told I could do better. By the time I went to secondary school my self-esteem was badly torn. By the time I left it was in tatters. Throughout my schooldays I was always looking for that someone. I suppose I was looking for someone who would be a mother to me.

We had Adoption Parades in the Orphanage in my earlier years. We would sit, neat and subdued in the playroom and adoptive parents would come and look us over. Most of the girls weren't available for adoption. I was, but people wanted pretty, cooing babies not plain, primary schoolchildren. These Parades died out before I left primary school but they left their mark on me.

The first "someone" was at Grammar School and I was eleven years old. Miss Merrivale taught geography and I tried very hard for her. I didn't have a "crush" on her; I just wanted her to like me. She was very gentle and kind. A year later she left to be a Sister of Mercy at Wantage. I was knocked sideways. How could anyone as nice as Miss Merrivale want to be a Sister of Mercy? I felt betrayed and Miss Merrivale went out of my life forever.

It wasn't until I went to boarding school at the age of fourteen that I found another "someone." Miss Roslyn was one of the matrons and she was young, pretty and kind-hearted. I had once written a poem at the Grammar School and Miss Roslyn fitted it exactly, I thought.

> I wish I had a mother
> Who was gentle, sweet and kind;
> I have a picture of her
> Oh so clearly in my mind;
> She has curly hair and laughing eyes
> And in them great affection lies;
> I wish I had a mother just like that.

I believed that I had found the mother I had wanted for so long. I used to see her whenever I could; I would help her with the laundry; I would do anything which gave me a few minutes with her. I would drop any girl I was with when Miss Roslyn came into view, which naturally led to quarrels. I didn't mind. I wanted to be with Miss Roslyn. I didn't often have anything wrong with me - I was pretty robust - but if I did, I prayed that Miss Roslyn would be on clinic duty. There were four matrons and they took it in turns.

One day during games I tripped and fell. I ran fast so the fall was a nasty one. I slid along the ground and took the skin off both legs. With the Orphanage training I got up and ran on, blood trickling down my legs. The game was almost at an end anyway so Miss Freedman, the games mistress, let it finish. She then sent me to the matron on duty. It was Miss Roslyn. This was no Sister Thelma with nail-brush and dry dressings. Miss Roslyn gently sponged both legs and washed away the blood. Then she carefully picked out the bits of gravel stuck in both legs. While she was working we talked of this and that - small talk to while away the time. I was just happy to be with her; to have her tend my wounds so gently.

The boarding school was for girls with little or no sight. Therefore we couldn't communicate in the usual way: smiling; sticking our noses in the air; turning away in an adolescent huff; sharing a silent joke with a sidelong glance. So we held hands, if we were friends. Blind girls held a sighted girl's arm anyway when we were somewhere strange. We also wrote letters to each other; we told each other the things we would have said with non-verbal communication. These letters might be acid; or they might be cordial. The cordial ones were usually written to our best friend or our "crush" of the moment. I only ever had one "crush" - Miss Roslyn. It wasn't a straightforward one either; it was complicated by my needing her as a mother figure and it lasted two years - far longer than other girls' "crushes" did.

I wrote long letters to Miss Roslyn. They weren't overly sentimental; they were about anything, everything - just to write to her. In the first term I told her in my letters that I was very glad that she was at school. I told her that I liked her and that I was very happy that she was there. I told her of my little successes and failures. I talked about everything except the Orphanage and wanting her to be my mother.

To each other we girls wrote in Braille. To Miss Roslyn, I wrote in code - the young teenager's love of secrecy. It was the current code of the time, which one of the girls had taught me, but I doubt whether Miss Roslyn ever ploughed through these letters. She had better things to do with her free time; she was courting.

The Christmas holidays came and I didn't want to go back to the Children's Home. (This was 1949 and the 1948 Act had been implemented by this time). I had been mercifully free of its cruelty and sadness for thirteen weeks and I didn't want to go back to it. Even less so now that Miss Roslyn had come into my life. I was very unhappy but I felt a little better when Miss Roslyn promised to write. I had her Christmas address and almost as soon as I got back to the Home I wrote to her. The letter was very long and very sentimental. I told her how much I needed a mother; how I missed her now that I was away from school; how I hated to be separated from her; how I knew she cared about me; nobody had ever cared about me before. And so on.

The letter was a voice crying in the wilderness. I got no answer. Nor any letter at all. I had taken a stamp back with me from school so Sister Penelope hadn't seen that letter. I had been able to post it secretly when I was sent on an errand.

I was very embarrassed about the letter when I got back to school. Part of me hoped that Miss Roslyn had never received it; the other part felt hurt and rejected. My dreams of having a mother were already fading and I avoided Miss Roslyn as much as possible.

A week or so into the term Miss Roslyn asked me why I hadn't written to thank her for the present she had sent. "I didn't get a present," I told her, "I didn't even get a letter. Did you get mine?" No, she hadn't. What a relief. I was finding out that it was one thing to write such a letter at a safe distance. It was quite another to have to face the receiver of it. What a puzzle. What had happened? The answer, when it came, was utterly awful.

In the Easter holidays Sister Penelope summoned me. On the Parlour desk was my letter to Miss Roslyn and her present to me. I had sent the letter to the wrong address - I had put 3 instead of 8 - and Miss Roslyn's present had arrived after I had gone back to school. My letter had been "returned to sender." Sister Penelope was very specific and very chilling. Normal people didn't write such letters. "How do you think she would have felt after getting this? This is the letter of a mentally disturbed person. It's just as well it never got there. People just don't write that sort of letter to each other." There was no "each other" about it. Miss Roslyn had never written to me. I was given the matron's present, with its Christmas note, and dismissed. Ironically, it was a small address book.

The encounter with Sister Penelope was all one way. There was no discussion as to why I might have wanted to write such a letter. I was angry, confused, embarrassed, humiliated and frightened. Angry because Sister Penelope read my letters; confused that it was abnormal to write that kind of letter; embarrassed that Sister Penelope had seen into my private thoughts and feelings; humiliated that she had been so dismissive of them; frightened that I was mad. It was the first loving letter I had ever written or received so I had no idea that it was abnormal. By that time Jessica had already gone to a mental hospital and I didn't want to go there too. I never wrote a loving letter like that again.

I never wrote to Miss Roslyn again in term-time either and my letters during the holidays were totally non-committal. I still sought her out and wanted to be with her, though. I was always hoping she would be that "someone-special." She never was. At the end of two years it was clear that she was getting fed up with it all. She never saw it as anything other than a "crush" and as I never dared mention "mothers" again she was never enlightened. At the end of my second year at boarding school Miss Roslyn left to get married. I tried to write to her and she wrote once or twice to me but it wasn't long before the letters stopped. I was incapable of writing to someone who had ceased to exist.

Miss Ellen, the Latin teacher, was my next "someone". This wasn't a crush. It was real need. I had learnt my lesson and didn't cling. Nor did I write to her about the longing inside me, acute though it was. I didn't want her to think I was mad. There was another restraining influence as well. Miss Ellen, being a teacher, had some say in our discipline and she was also stern in her teaching. If we made too many mistakes in our homework we did it again - in detention. I spent quite a lot of time in detention and it was like being back in the Home. It reinforced my sense of worthlessness and failure. It is true that I didn't cling but it is also true that I left friends flat if I saw Miss Ellen - to talk about Horace or Tacitus and suchlike. The girls that I left standing were, again, offended but I was looking for Eldorado. I was trying to build a relationship with someone I didn't see very often and who had no idea of the depth of my need.

I saw Miss Ellen in Latin lessons, in the dining room when she was on duty and in detention when she came to check on us. The only time I saw her to really speak to was when I engineered it but that wasn't possible very often. No-one else really mattered. It became much easier later on because Miss Ellen was great friends with Mrs Heymann, the school's administrator.

Mrs Heymann and her two daughters had escaped from Germany in the nick of time before World War II, as had two or three other refugees from Europe on the staff. As Miss Ellen spent quite a lot of time in Mrs Heymann's office I saw her much more often.

As I got to know Mrs Heymann better I used to go and talk to her. I couldn't talk to her much about the Children's Home but I could tell her about school troubles - and there were plenty of those. Our talks together and Mrs Heymann's warmth and care started a relationship which grew into a lifelong friendship with her and her two daughters.

On the other hand, two incidents were to prevent Miss Ellen ever becoming that "someone- special". Once, before a job interview in my final school year, I went with Miss Ellen to her home. I didn't know it then but she had elderly parents. I remember almost nothing of that visit; not even how long I was there. I remember only one thing but that one thing was significant. Without any explanation, Miss Ellen bade me wait in the sitting room and I was there for some time. There could have been a hundred reasons why it was more convenient for me to wait but for me it had only one meaning - Children's Home - and it undermined my trust in Miss Ellen. I had spent too much time outside the parlour door, up in my cell or, later, in my attic room expecting punishment of some sort and for years afterwards I could never bide my time anywhere in peace and tranquillity. It was always tainted with a sense of foreboding. In any case, the relationship with Miss Ellen, such as it was, came to an abrupt halt. We had an argument over Mother Church. Miss Ellen was a convinced and practising Christian, while I was already a firm disbeliever. I had reason to state my disbelief but I couldn't tell Miss Ellen why. She knew almost nothing about the Children's Home or Sisters of Mercy so she didn't understand my rejection of religion. She said she was scandalised that I had rejected Mother Church - the Church which had nurtured me since babyhood. Miss Ellen would never know what those words did to me; only their effect. Blast off. Another relationship gone.

At the same time as Miss Ellen came into my life I was looking for my real mother. Even as a child I had had dreams about my mother. My parents were wonderful people and one day they would come. I half-knew they wouldn't but I went on dreaming. The worst nightmare of my childhood involved my parents and it was a very frequent one. I would be called to the Parlour, expecting trouble but there were my mother and father. I knew them immediately. My mother would reach out to me and take me in her arms. They had found me at last. We all three sat and smiled and smiled. Then I would reach out to hug my mother again but she wasn't there. Both my parents had disappeared. I would call to them, broken-hearted, but there would be no answer. I would wake up with my hands tied to the bed or, later, I would wake up with my arms wrapped round myself, tears running down my cheeks. The deep longing within me wouldn't let me believe that they were never going to come. They wanted to come but couldn't - this, in spite of no letter, no card, no visit - no nothing.

In my mid-teens I asked Miss Russell where my mother was and what she was like. In a letter Miss Russell told me that my mother wasn't the best of all possible mothers. However, she gave me the address of my mother's sister and I wrote to my aunt occasionally. After a while I plucked up my courage and arranged to go and stay with her in the hope that I could see my mother. I was four weeks off my sixteenth birthday. I didn't tell Sister Penelope until the trip was fixed up because I didn't think she would let me go. For one thing, she didn't like me going to stay even with my school-friends. She had already written to one girl's mother to refuse an invitation.

She told Pam's mother that I was needed in the holidays to look after the children.

Sister Penelope was very serious when I got back in the holidays. She had bought my ticket but she wasn't happy about the trip. "You realise that if your mother wants to take you back there's nothing we can do about it. You were never legally bound over to us." Everyone had obviously been so certain that my mother wouldn't come looking for me that they hadn't bothered with the niceties. Sister Penelope's gravity - where I had expected anger - should have warned me but all I could think was: Whoever would choose to stay in The Haven?

I set off with high hopes. I was going to meet my own mother; my aunt had managed to arrange it. When I arrived I found that my aunt lived in a big house, in multi-occupation with several more of my aunts and uncles. These were my family but I felt nothing at all. They were, and have remained, strangers. I don't even know to which side of the family they belonged. I couldn't understand why I didn't feel happy with these relations of mine. The house seemed to be full of sorrow, fighting and acrimony. I was already het up and all this made me feel miserable and afraid. None of it fitted in with my dreams but none of it could compare with what followed.

On the day we were supposed to go and see my mother my aunt got a letter. "Bill (my stepfather) doesn't want us to go over there." said my aunt. The world lurched to a halt. "Don't worry," said my aunt, "she can come over here." and I went through the agony of waiting all over again. On the appointed day my mother wouldn't come. She offered no reason or alternative. Full stop. Period. End of conversation. My hopes and dreams crashed down around my feet. I was chucked back with a jolt into the heap of rubble out of which I thought I was climbing. "Never mind," said my aunt, "We'll go and see your gran." - my aunt's mother. We went. My aunt and her mother hugged and kissed each other and, while watching them, I thought of what might have been. I didn't feel like a grand-daughter. I drank tea and made the right sort of noises until it was time to go. I was in a state of extreme shock and utter wretchedness. I couldn't get away from the awful truth. It was stark. My mother didn't want me. Even worse, my three brothers were living with her.

I wrote and asked Sister Penelope to find a reason for me to go back early. Sister Penelope wrote and said I had to go back for an appointment at the orthopaedic clinic. I sent her the time of arrival of the bus and two days later I left the place of my dreams and went back to the rubble.

Better to be back in the Home, where anger and violence would stifle the hurt; annul the grief. I don't remember anything of the journey back. I was drowning in a sea of anguish. I got back to the Home just after tea. Sister Penelope was "down" and Sister Annette was surprised to see me. "Whatever are you doing back so early? We weren't expecting you. Tea's finished and your bed isn't made." she said. Light words but they emphasised my nothingness. I belonged nowhere and to no-one. The words snipped a few more strands of my dangerously short tether. "I don't want any bloody tea." I muttered and dragged myself upstairs. I just reached my room as the dam burst. My room was a bed-sized cell between two dormitories, very small but private: I fell onto the bare, lumpy mattress and sank into a bottomless pit. That night I went down to Hell. Hours later, when I stopped crying, I was wrung dry and totally empty.

Neither of the Sisters asked me if I wanted to talk about the episode. Counselling wasn't a part of Child Care in those days. By the same token, I told them nothing that mattered about the visit. "You in your small corner and I in mine."

A fortnight later my "gran" sent me a photo and a letter. In the photograph my mother has her hands protectively on the shoulders of a little girl; my half-sister. The letter was three months old. I still have it. As I read it the knife turned and turned.

My Dear Mum and all,
Peggy (my little half-sister) was ill, about a fortnight before Xmas and ... taken to hospital Jan. 16th. Ever since I have been going to work a few hrs in the morning, and straight to hospital until 5 & 6 o'clock in the evening, she has been very ill and the danger is not yet over. I hope I am never called on to go through such hell again.
I did not have a bite in my lips for nearly a fortnight during

the very worst... if I crack up the bab will be worse off as the doctors and nurses say that things might not have been so good if I hadn't been with her so much..."

I never had anything more to do with my family. Sixteen years of nothing. All my searching for a stand-in mother had failed and I had felt rejected and unwanted. Now my real mother didn't want me. I felt totally abandoned.

The following year a small baby of eight months came to the Home. This was during the summer holidays and I was detailed to look after it. What a bore. I hated babies. When I actually started though, it was quite different and my attitude changed. No-one wanted to look after the baby; she was much too difficult. I called her Pudding. At first Pudding was totally non-reactive. I could only get food down her by shovelling it into her mouth. She swallowed some and spat the rest out. I worked hard. I tickled her; I played This Little Piggy. Nothing. I talked non-stop and chucked her under the chin. Nothing. I took her out in the pushchair; I joggled her up and down kerbs. Nothing. One day I joggled it a bit too hard and Pudding bumped her head on the upright. Nothing. I was more upset than she was. Contrite, I gave her a flower from the hedgerow. She dropped it unnoticed. I couldn't understand it. I was confused. I'd never seen a baby like this.

Gradually, oh, so very gradually, Pudding began to respond and by the end of the summer holidays we had made great progress. When the time came to go I didn't want to leave Pudding. She was my baby. I went back to school, for once looking forward to the Christmas holidays. Christmas came and excitedly I went back to the Home. I looked for Pudding straightaway but she was gone. I was shattered. Had Pudding's mother come and taken away my baby? How dared she!

Sister Annette told me that Pudding had gone away. "Where to?" I asked but Sister Annette wouldn't say. Later, Rosie told me that she was dead. Broncho-pneumonia, they said. I was heart-broken but I hid my wrenching grief and emptiness deep inside me. One day it welled up and I cried. Crying was something I just didn't do, usually. Sister Annette found me crying and, with great surprise, asked me why. Eventually, I foolishly told her. "Don't be so sloppy," she scoffed, " anyone would think she was your baby." She was! She was! I cried out silently. ·For one long summer holiday we had spoken to each other's need. What did Sister Annette know of that?

These griefs and hurts and wounds couldn't be discussed with the other girls. It needed a wiser head. We couldn't talk to the wielder of the cat-o'four-tails; nor to the destroyer with the tongue. Who could we turn to for help? The Sisters had no inkling of our deepest needs, or if they had they never showed it. Often, in moments of emotional distress, they were hostile. As with Pudding. Or the time when I trod on the rabbit and Sister Penelope called me a clumsy fool. They didn't understand so we hid those moments deeper. When my mother brushed me aside and crushed me there was no-one to put me together again. There was never anyone. Like a volcano, the seething pressures built up. Like a volcano, we coughed fire and sulphur. Jessica threw the shoes at Sister Annette. Polly got tired of endlessly sweeping the leaves against the wind and one day she hit Sister Annette with the yard broom, dashed inside and locked Sister Annette out. We all silently cheered.

Like a volcano we sometimes erupted. I was 18 years old. The time was the summer holidays before my last year at school. The year was 1953 and I was in the kitchen writing a letter. Sister Penelope came in and asked me to go on an errand. It wasn't urgent and I would be able to post the letter. I looked up and said: "Yes, all right, just let me finish this letter." I only had the "goodbye" to write. I had no intention of being rude but Sister Penelope exploded. "You get up and do it now," she stormed. "You're getting too cocky by half." The staff at boarding school didn't do this sort of thing and the letter could already have been finished. The volcano began to smoke. I didn't get up. I, too, was getting angry. I sped through the red light. "That's the trouble with this bloody place." I fumed, "You can never finish a damn thing in peace." We were heading for disaster.

Sister Penelope was furious. "I shall write to your headmistress ..." A fatal error. The last straw. My self-control snapped and I didn't let her finish. "For chrissake write to her then and see if I care." I was well into the danger zone. Throughout my whole life someone had been writing to someone about me. It drove me mad and I felt threatened by it. It was like being covered with cobwebs and I was sick of it all. Sister Penelope was coming across the kitchen. She looked menacing. "You're asking for a good hiding, my girl." I knew I would get it, too, if I gave her half a chance. Suddenly, sixteen and a half years of suppression, of abuse, of one crisis after another, of dammed-up feelings and pent-up emotions rose in my gorge. The volcano erupted.

"All right then, come and get me. If you want a fight you can have it." I came out of my chair like a cannon ball and hurled myself at Sister Penelope. She was twice my size but I was beyond caution. I was also very frightened. I had never seen Sister Penelope in such a towering rage. She struck out at me but I dodged and threw a wild punch at her. I wanted to crush her. I don't remember much about the next few seconds. When I came back to normal, Sister Penelope had her back to the kitchen range, her head hard up against the top edge of the range recess, her back arched away from it. Luckily, she was a tall woman. I was holding her wrists and the knotted veins in her hands were swollen and standing out. I pushed away from her and backed off to the table. I knew it was finished - for that time anyway. Reaction had set in and I was shivering uncontrollably. Underneath my new-found sense of power there was alarm and deep misgiving. I knew the shocking truth that in that moment of white-hot fury I could have killed Sister Penelope. I was sent to Dr Graham-Campbell, as usual after such set-tos. He could find nothing wrong and ordered a tonic, which went down the sink in plausible doses.

Sister Penelope also feared for my immortal soul. In the Christmas term following the set-to she wrote to the head mistress and asked if I made Confession on a regular basis? Sister Penelope hadn't worried before so I had got away with not doing it for the last four years. "No," I told the head mistress, who was a fervent Roman Catholic. "I don't believe in it any more and it would be living a lie." The head mistress said it might help to keep the peace if I went. How could I do something so fundamentally wrong just to keep the peace?

I went to the priest appointed for the task of bringing me back to the fold. I was totally on the defensive. "I'm here because I'm in enough trouble already. I've been told to come but I don't want to come any more. I don't believe in God. I can cope with the services to save trouble but not Confession. That would be too much of a lie." I was as prickly as a cactus.

"Better not to then, if you feel like that." said the priest mildly, "Why don't we just talk instead." I stared at him. How odd. The Convent chaplain wouldn't have said that, I thought. We talked.

It was early in the term when I first went to him. On that occasion we talked generally of belief and unbelief. The second time the priest tried to draw me out. I was very reluctant so we talked generally again. He was very understanding. Later I found that he was also deeply compassionate. He didn't force any issues. He trod very delicately. Above all, he knew I needed to talk. To encourage me, he said: "You do realise, don't you, that what you say to me here is bound by the silence of the Confessional." "But I'm not really making my Confession, am I?" I was suspicious and mistrustful of everyone by this time. I wouldn't have trusted a chicken to lay an egg. "You are, in a sense," he said, "and what you say to me here is in the strictest confidence." "You won't believe me." "We could try." he suggested gently, "It might help you to talk."

I went to him about six times in all during that year. He wasn't always there and I wouldn't go to anyone else. When the priest was away I used to go to a fairly secluded cafe, where I had a quiet coffee and went back to school at the appropriate hour.

We talked of missing people; cruelty; how God and the Devil worked against us; how meaningless hymns and prayers were; how Christians said one thing in Church and did quite another outside. All the things which disturbed me about life in general and religion in particular. These were quiet discussions. They always started and ended with a prayer. When the priest first suggested it I thought: "Here we go. Mouthing words." I wasn't going to listen but I did. They weren't empty prayers. They were his own and he said them by himself. He didn't ask me to join in. He didn't tell me to close my eyes and fold my hands. I wasn't aggressive about not doing it. I just didn't. We didn't kneel. Gradually, carefully, he taught me that we created God in our own image. God wasn't savage. Nor was He necessarily responsible for the way we behaved. Even more slowly, I took him spiritually into The Haven.

I know he believed me. He didn't just leave me to ramble on. He asked questions and we explored my answers. I asked him questions and we discussed his responses. That priest was a first-class counsellor long before they were the fashion and he gave me far more help even than he realised.

Chapter 9

The Path to Freedom

".. to undo the heavy burdens, and to let
the oppressed go free...

Isaiah, 1ii, 7

As a child I always wanted to know everything. "How, where, when, why?" Mouldy Cheese and Aggy Ragbag couldn't hope to maintain the Lesser Silence while the other girls were at school. They gave me picture books to look at. Lupins, larkspur, nasturtiums, dahlias. They must have been flower catalogues. I loved the masses of colourful flowers and I asked the Sisters endless questions about them. They gave me Children's Worship to look at. This was the service of Matins and it had pictures; Mary gazing at her baby; Christ floating up to heaven. The writing was in chunks of blue and red; the priest's words were in red, the congregation's in blue. I knew what our words were; I had said them so often in church.

Before I went to school I could read Children's Worship fluently but I don't remember anyone ever teaching me. I went to Primary School at the age of five years and four months and when we were given a book to read I read it. It was very simple. I had nearly finished it when, like a lightning strike, I got a resounding slap on my leg. "You haven't even got the right page." said the class teacher crossly. She went back a few pages. "What does that say?" She pointed. I was crying. What had I done wrong? I was trying very hard. I liked school. Sniffling, I read the words. Miss Chambers, our teacher, turned to the next page. "What does that say?" I told her. She did this three or four times, then she said: "You'd better go and play in the sand pit." I was in disgrace but I didn't know why.

I went to the sand pit. I had a big red hand mark on my left leg. I knew I was being punished but I liked playing in the sandpit. I could draw, write or build and it was fun. The only thing I wasn't allowed to do was talk. Whenever we had reading lessons I had to go to the sand pit. It took me some time to realise why; I could read and the others couldn't. I was "different" but I didn't know why.

One difference was my eyes. I was the only one who had to sit in the front row to be able to see the blackboard. I was the only one who had to hold a book right up to my face to see it. I was the only one who couldn't see when the light was dim or it was dark. That was a fault in me, I knew; Sister Thelma was already teaching me that.

Then the boys at school started to bully me. "Four eyes, four eyes." "Boss-eyed, boss-eyed." They used to crowd behind me, chanting nasty things. There were four particular ones and they were all bigger than me but not as big as Sister Thelma. I was already terrified of her but I wasn't afraid of the boys. One day they provoked me too far. I'd had enough. "You say that again I'll bash you." I said, probably copying someone else's threat. Two or three days later they started again. No further warning. I turned and punched the biggest boy on his nose. I was already used to fighting my corner and was ready to go on but I didn't have to. The boy's nose was bleeding and the duty teacher had arrived. The boy was taken away and cleaned up and the others had drifted away. No-one ever bullied me again.

I loved everything about school; spelling, mental arithmetic, composition, knitting - especially the teacher who knitted the first and last stitches of each row for me. Above all, we were away from the Orphanage for much of the day - though not always far enough. The teachers lived close by and sometimes told the Sisters of our misdemeanours. Or we could be in trouble for fighting, especially if we bore the marks of it when we returned from school. My glasses often got broken in fights or from falls. When they were, a broken lens would be taken right out; a cracked lens would be stuck with sticky paper. If it were the left lens out or blocked, I could use the right eye comfortably. When the right eye was out of action it was murder because I could never see very well with the left eye. There is much less sight in it than in the right and if the right eye is blocked, the left one moves uncontrollably. Seeing anything clearly is quite impossible.

In the Top Class - the last year at Primary School - we were prepared for the Scholarship. We spent each afternoon doing all sorts of tests and puzzles - finding the missing word or number; the odd one in a series of pictures; spelling, mental arithmetic. I have always liked puzzles, solving problems and so on so I was in my element. I wanted so much to pass the Scholarship and go to the Grammar School. No-one from the Orphanage had ever been there so it was a mystery. More than that, we would be away from the Orphanage all day. It was only dream-time though. We orphans wouldn't be allowed to take the Scholarship, I felt sure. Sometimes we took work or pictures back to the Orphanage after school but we had to throw them in the rubbish bin. "We don't want all that paper cluttering up the playroom," said the Sisters. Even our good work was "rubbish." I soon believed that it wasn't any good, even if the teacher said it was. After a few times I stopped taking commended work back to the Orphanage.

The head master, Mr Parsons, was class teacher for the Top Class. One day he asked: "Who will be eleven by such-and-such a date? They will take the Scholarship this year. Hands up, all of you". Mabel and I didn't put our hands up. Mr Parsons looked at me. "When are you eleven, Joan?" "May, Sir, but please Sir, I'm an orphan." Mr Parsons smiled "Orphans can take the Scholarship. Put your hand up - and you Mabel." I raised my hand a little way but not too far. I was afraid that this magic would go away if I did.

From that day on I thought of nothing else. I worked even harder at puzzles and compositions. I had to pass the Scholarship if I wanted to go to the Grammar School.

Sister Annette, recently arrived, began to call Mabel and me Lady Muck and the other girls copied her. We were the first orphans to benefit from the 1944 Education Act. "All children should be educated according to age, ability and aptitude." None of us knew that then. What the other girls did know was that we were getting a chance they hadn't had. Understandably, it didn't go down very well. In their place I would have felt the same.

Came the day. The Scholarship examination was just like all the afternoons of the previous months and I loved it. All my favourite puzzles, the same sort of arithmetic and spelling, a nice composition. Afterwards, I was bubbling over. "Wasn't it nice," I said as we came out. What a mistake. I didn't know then that not everyone likes examinations and that I shouldn't have said I enjoyed it, even though I had. The other girls didn't speak to me very much for a while. They went on calling me Lady Muck but not Mabel. I had punched her on the nose by that time.

Secretly I hoped I had done well enough to pass. By the time the results came Mabel had gone home. That morning there was great excitement in the playground. Two girls knew that they had passed the Scholarship. No-one had told me anything so I supposed that I hadn't passed. My dreams were in ruins. There was to be no Grammar School for me. Well, who cared anyway? I wanted to cry but by this time I had learnt not to show my feelings. The half-open door of freedom had slammed shut in my face. Didn't that always happen to orphans? The other orphans at school knew I hadn't passed and they were nice to me. Their turn hadn't come yet. We went into Morning Assembly. After prayers the announcement was made but I wasn't really listening. It wasn't for me. I was trying hard to look as if I didn't care.

"... three successful candidates."

Three? We only knew of two. There was a buzz of excitement. "They are..." Everyone was quiet. Mr Parsons looked at the Top Class row. It was agony. "Maureen Sharpe ... Daphne Morris ... Mr Parsons smiled at both. His eyes moved on and I waited for him to pass me over but he stopped and smiled, "... and Joan Hall."

I was stunned. The Grammar School beckoned. Me? Really? I was going to the Grammar School after all? My dreams started again and I heard almost nothing after that. At playtime I joined the other orphans but I wasn't really one of them any longer. Maureen and Daphne didn't help by looking for me more and more in the playground. Sister Annette went on calling me Lady Muck and the other girls followed suit. It hurt but none of them knew. "You'll soon be expelled from there," said Sister Annette scathingly. "They won't want to keep you at the Grammar School." I didn't understand. At school on Friday afternoons we had silent reading and I had read books about girls who got expelled for doing really bad things at school. I hadn't even been to Grammar School yet. Would orphans just be expelled? I was frightened. It's hard to pretend not to care and bravado seems like showing off. Sister Annette called me stuck up and the girls did the same for a while. We were kinder to each other than Sister Annette was to us though. At first we would go along with the bullying, then we'd feel sorry for the girl who was being picked on and we would start being nice to her again. Sometimes Sister Annette could be kind but that was confusing. We couldn't always tell whether she was really being kind or whether it was just malice. She began saying that I would probably marry Professor Huffen-Puffen (pronounced like "put") and become famous but it never quite sounded like a joke.

Grammar School needs a whole new uniform and one day in the holidays Sister Monica took me to Markham's the school outfitter, to get it. I had never been to buy clothes before. We always wore donated hand-me-downs from a pool of clothes in the Orphanage. Shoes, also hand-me-downs, came out of the shoe cupboard, so an outing to buy a whole new set of clothes was nothing short of a miracle.

Markham's smelt of new clothes and the smell was overpowering. I gazed in wonder at the blouses, gym-slips and blazers all hanging invitingly about the shop. I took deep breaths to absorb the exciting smells as Sister Monica pulled me over to the counter. As the uniform was assembled piece by piece I buried my face in the clothes. The smell was intoxicating. Sister Monica pulled me away. "Whatever do you think you are doing? You mustn't do things like that." The woman smiled at me and began packing it all up. I watched very closely, afraid that she would leave something out.

We started back to the Orphanage and I insisted on carrying the parcel, heavy though it was. Sister Monica was talking as if I were suddenly older and, as we walked, I gradually plucked up my courage. There was something I wanted to know and I probably wouldn't get another chance to ask. Suddenly the question burst out. "Sister, where's my father and mother?" Sister Monica's step faltered for an instant. Then she set off again, almost too fast for me to keep up. "Don't you worry about your parents. You're much better off where you are." I tried to get Sister Monica to talk about it but she refused point-blank. I had ruined the outing. I said not another word. Why were my parents such a secret?

I wouldn't speak to Sisters Annette or Monica when we got back so Sister Monica finally sent me away. "I thought Joan had given up this habit of not answering. I expect the Grammar School's gone to her head..." said Sister Monica. I was very angry. Sister Monica knew it was her fault for not telling me about my parents. It had nothing to do with Grammar School. Grown-ups were always making things up. What was the matter with my parents? Why couldn't I be with them? Why was I better off in the Orphanage?

As always at such times, a red light began to glow. I was being driven towards it by a force inside me over which I had no control. The pressure began to build. For her refusal to tell me about my parents I brought my guns to bear on Sister Monica. For several days I wouldn't answer her until just before she reached explosion point. It was a game I knew well how to play by this time and playing it reduced a lot of tension. The red light grew brighter.

I played the game time and time again and take-off got nearer and nearer. The red light was dazzling. I ignored it and pushed Sister Monica to the limit. She was a mild-mannered person, even if she did like giving Holy Lectures, but when at last she blew she went into orbit. She stripped me naked verbally and finished by threatening early expulsion from Grammar School. "They won't put up with this kind of behaviour." she warned. "You can now go up to bed for the rest of the day. You will have plenty of time to think about mending your ways." I slouched out of the room to show how little I cared, then climbed unhappily into bed. The day stretched a long way into the future of night-time. I was too old at eleven to play with stamps and anyway I didn't feel like playing. I was by myself and I cried. I cried because I wanted to be out walking with the others; I cried because I'd brought it on myself; I cried because I still didn't know about my parents and because Sister Monica didn't seem to understand. She said I was better off without them. I cried even harder because I could never ask again. I cried because I was going to be expelled. I hated the whole world.

x   x   x   x   x   x

Grammar School started well. I was very respectful, very polite, very quiet. I mustn't do anything to get expelled, I thought. At lunch-time I sat by myself in the shade of a tree, trying to adjust to the strange and confusing idea of not having a job to do. I told myself that I was going to do well. In class I sat in the front row so that I would be able to see the blackboard. I had done that at Primary School and it had been all right. The teachers there had written in big, clear letters with thick, white chalk. At Grammar School it wasn't too bad at first. There was very little on the board and blackboard writing, like many other things, fills the space available. It was therefore often quite big and readable. When I couldn't read it, I copied off Theresa, my neighbour, if possible. We got told off for talking so it wasn't always very easy, especially as it could get us bad marks against our House.

I didn't want to get into trouble so I was very careful and managed to survive. I got high marks in the monthly tests and my end-of-term reports were good. I loved games and swimming and did well. In fact, I often stayed behind after school for games practice as there was some talk of my being in the school hockey and netball teams. My main problem was having to cope with being odd man out both at school and in the Orphanage. In the Orphanage, I had homework, I went to school alone and I was often home late.

I wasn't able to play with the others because of homework. This I did in a room where I could hear the other children and once the novelty of having homework wore off I wanted to be part of them again. I felt lonely and isolated. As we were not allowed out in the evening I couldn't visit my schoolfriends or join in weekend events. I had very little pocket money so I couldn't buy treats when the others did. I didn't get rewards for gaining House Points - notable events. My classmates usually showed us what parents or other family members had given them when they did. I wasn't jealous; that was part of life for us orphans; it was just that I didn't have anything to display and it embarrassed me. The girls also talked about the latest films, records and so on. I couldn't and I felt left out. Would I ever fit in anywhere? In work and play, though, I was more than holding my own. My end-of-year exam results were good. I was on my way. To where?

The second year started badly and went downhill all the way. The first two or three weeks were all right because Mavis and I were getting ready to go into hospital to have our hammer toes straightened. We went in on October 9th and came out on November 23rd. Some work was brought to us in hospital from school and there was a hospital teacher but neither was really sufficient so we were behind when we went back to school at the beginning of December. Also, I found that in the second year there was more writing on the blackboard and it was smaller and fainter. I couldn't read very much of it and that meant copying more from Theresa.

Our form mistress was less easy going than in the first year and Theresa and I went to the head mistress three times in about five weeks. I stopped copying from Theresa after that; it wasn't fair to her. Even with Theresa's help I had often missed a key point so then I couldn't make proper sense of a lesson; without, it was much worse. Theresa was a loyal friend and I had sworn her to secrecy. In our world in those days there was no such thing as "leaks"; a promise given was a promise kept. Theresa couldn't understand why I wouldn't tell anyone but I couldn't explain - I was too ashamed of the fault in me - and Theresa kept her word.

At the same time we were trying to cope with the changes in the Orphanage. Sister Eleanor had taken the place of Sister Annette and Sister Penelope had replaced Sister Monica. The new, harsher regime was in place but discipline was disintegrating. No amount of punishment, however severe, could halt its collapse and there were several visits to the Parlour for me. They changed nothing. Nor did the headmistress's letters about my schoolwork. I sometimes went to school with stripes on my thighs or bruises on my body. When I did, I "missed" my usual train if our first lesson was gym - another reason for letters but even that was better than anyone seeing the marks on me. In the Orphanage we got more and more out of hand - then the four of us went on the rampage. During those weeks of rioting I got no homework done at all but it didn't seem to matter anyway. I wasn't taking in the lessons well enough to do justice to my homework. Like the Gadarene swine I was in headlong flight towards self-destruction.

Then Sister Annette came back. The reins were put on us and pulled tight. Sister Annette's tongue was sharpened and we were back under control. I started to do my homework again, Theresa let me copy her notes from her books and, slowly, I dragged myself back from the brink. My Easter term report was marginally better than the Christmas one but not much. Luckily, I was born with an IQ of 140 and a flair for languages; otherwise all would have been lost. My IQ helped me to make some sense of new work - with the added support of Theresa's notes. My love of languages helped me to make good in those subjects and fortunately they didn't involve too much close board work. In the Easter holidays I worked solidly through my text books and managed to get a reasonable grasp of missed work.

One area where I had no trouble was in sport - well, not with the sports themselves. Otherwise I seemed to have a genius for creating trouble where it didn't exist. It wasn't actually genius though; more crass stupidity. In the summer term some of us took to playing cricket in the lunch hour and that gave me a brilliant idea. We skipped lunch so that we had longer to play and as I wasn't having lunch, I thought I needn't pay my dinner money. Oh dear. Trouble all round and letters in all directions. "It isn't your money, anyway." Sister Penelope said angrily. "If you can't be trusted with it I'll have to send it. Is that clear?" How humiliating.

I tried once more to self-destruct that term. Towards the end of term we had a swimming gala. The four School Houses competed against each other and I was in two events. I was really looking forward to the gala. Swimming doesn't need good eyesight and I loved it. I revelled in the rhythm and co-ordination; the sense of my body powering through the water. I relished cutting the water with a dive and swimming under water. When I surfaced, I felt I had left all my troubles on the bottom.

The games mistress was our form mistress that year and she had arranged a friendly netball match amongst ourselves the day after the gala. The match was to be followed by a camp fire picnic in her garden, with sausages, chips and other delights. Sister Penelope had already given me permission to go on the picnic so I didn't mention the gala to her when I knew I was competing in it. I still wasn't getting any prizes for good behaviour and the tensions in the Orphanage weren't helping. Retribution could be very strange with Sister Penelope in charge. We would be punished for an offence, real or imagined. We would then pay another penalty, totally unexpected, for the same offence. The dinner money episode had happened not long before the gala and I thought that Sister Penelope would therefore allow only one event: the gala or the picnic. Anyway, I thought that the gala would finish within the normal afternoon span. When the day came I dropped my swimming togs out of the window into our alley and as I was always the first one out no-one knew.

The best-laid plans ... The gala went on well into the evening. I was too worried to do as well as I should have done in the relay - the last race - thus causing grave displeasure. As soon as it had finished I scrambled to the changing room, dragged my clothes on and raced to the station - to see the train pulling out. I ran the half mile to the bus-stop but the bus was already going out of sight round the corner. There was no further need to hurry. I walked back to the railway station and caught the 8.15 p.m. train with time to spare and to think about the consequences. No excuse would do. I was altogether too late and without permission. I walked slowly up our street. The tension was building and my thigh muscles were twitching, my legs turning to jelly. I passed two women, standing at their doors enjoying the excitement. "They've got the p'lice out looking for you." they told me with undisguised enjoyment. I wasn't worried about the police. Polly was often at the station and she didn't seem to be afraid of them. I was much more afraid of what all the gefuffle was doing to Sister Penelope's temper and right arm.

I got to the Orphanage a few minutes after nine o'clock. I hardly dared to pull on the bell. It clanged in the hall like the summons to Hades. Sister Penelope opened the door and I flattened myself against the wall as I went through the door. "Where have you been?" she asked quietly - too quietly. I told her. "Go up to your room". I backed away, then turned and scampered up the stairs. I sat, fully clothed, on my bed and listened. No footsteps yet. Where was she? I waited ... Perhaps she was telling the police I was back. I listened...

No-one came. She must be locking up. It couldn't take that long. I waited... I got undressed and put on my nightie. She would strip me anyway. Less to take off. I lay down and waited ... I wished she would hurry up and get it over. It was the waiting which was so nerve-racking. Once she started it was already on the way to being over. Perhaps she was saying Compline. It was said at 9 p.m. and the Great Silence followed.

I suddenly realised that Sister Penelope couldn't lay hands on me after Compline. The Greater Silence ... Was she waiting till tomorrow? Eventually I fell asleep. I didn't get a thrashing the next day. I didn't go to the picnic either. Instead I did "hard labour." - polishing and scrubbing. I would much rather have had the physical punishment, though terrible it would have been, I thought. Missing the picnic was a far worse penalty ... As I scrubbed it dawned on me that if I had been whipped and allowed to go to the netball game and picnic, how would I have hidden the stripes?

I didn't do at all well in the end-of-year exams. All that can be said is that I didn't fail.

x x x x x x

My third year at Grammar School began and I was still facing downhill. I was in so much trouble both at the Orphanage and at school that I didn't dare to say anything about the blackboard. I didn't want to get into any more trouble - my sense of right and wrong was completely haywire by this time. I was trying hard but not getting anywhere. Letters were beginning to pass between school, the Wiltshire Education Authority and the Orphanage. I had to improve dramatically and immediately or I would be out. (I wrote to the Wiltshire Education Authority in 1996 to ask if they had any record of all this but, regrettably, they only keep files for five years after a pupil leaves school).

Threatening rumblings were getting louder on all sides. Sister Penelope was warning me to pull my socks up or else. Teachers were doing the same. At the beginning of the Easter term the headmistress issued a stern formal warning. "Improve forthwith or you must go. The Wiltshire Education Authority won't go on paying for you unless you do." Fear of expulsion robbed me of what little sense I had left. Sister Penelope told me exactly what she thought of me: I was a disgrace to the Orphanage; I had wasted a good opportunity; I was a thoroughly bad lot; I was scruffy; (In the dark I was always falling over, holing my stockings and dirtying my tunic); The Orphanage would never be able to send another girl to the Grammar School I was at; (They didn't. Two to three years later, the next girl went to a Grammar School in the opposite direction) you couldn't make silk purses out of sow's ears; she was very disappointed in me... and so on.

Everyone was disappointed in me. They always were. I was scatty with fright. I had to do something. A few days later, very hesitantly, I approached the form-mistress. "Please," I said, "I can't see the blackboard. I'm sorry. I do try." I was trying not to cry. Miss Urwin was speechless. She looked at the offending board. It was covered with her neat, small writing.

In the afternoon I went with Miss Urwin to the headmistress. She too was almost bereft of words. "Why ever didn't you tell us?" she asked, totally at a loss to understand. How could I explain? I looked at my shoes instead. Suddenly everyone wanted to help me. Nobody could fathom why I hadn't told them in my first term at school and I could never enlighten them. Notes were made for me. I could copy from Theresa. I could go and look at the board. I made great strides.

More letters between school, Wiltshire Education Authority and the Children's Home. This time the subject was a Special School, opened twenty eight years previously but I had first to see an eye specialist. He had me registered as partially sighted and an entrance test in the summer term secured me a place at Chorleywood College "For Girls With Little or no Sight".

Chorleywood College was a boarding school and I started there in September 1949. I was 14 years old. In four months my world had started turning in a totally different direction. When I left the Grammar School my classmates made a little collection for me. I was overwhelmed. They had been told that I was going blind and their spontaneous gesture warmed my heart. I didn't tell the Sisters. I was afraid that they would take the money away.

Chorleywood is in the glorious countryside of Hertfordshire and the College was on the edge of the Common. In the late '80s it was amalgamated with the Royal Worcester College for Boys. A large part of the grounds was taken up by two Sportex pitches, Sportex being a game specially designed for our school. It had elements of rounders, hockey, cricket and rugby and it was played with a white netball. Both blind and sighted girls played it. There was also a tennis court and tennis too was played with a netball, though the normal rules applied. Then there was swimming. We had our own pool.

Exercise played a very important part in the school curriculum. We had gymnastics and eurhythmics - which we called Greek Flops because we wore Greek-style tunics. Every day, between two and three p.m. we went for compulsory walks. Until the Upper Fourth form we went in crocodile; then we could go in pairs, our partner being a blind girl. On the first warm, sunny day in the Easter term we would have the Spring Walk. There were three walks, short, medium and long. We set off after breakfast and I loved walking through the wakening natural world. I always chose to go on the long walk. I loved all forms of sport and exercise - except Greek Flops.

Braille was used for all reading and writing and German was also compulsory. As I knew neither I was to repeat the Upper Fourth year. That was a very good idea, I thought. By repeating that year I could catch up on what I had missed at the Grammar School. For the first six weeks I only joined the class for German, otherwise I was learning to read and write Braille.

Braille is based on six dots:

```
1   .   .   4
2   .   .   5
3   .   .   6
```

Learning Braille, therefore, means starting with the alphabet. Different combinations of dots stand for different letters; for instance, dots 2, 3 and 4 = S. Most letters also stand for a word. S = so;   with dot 5 before it,   S = some. Various dots in front of letters stand for groups of letters. For example, dot 6 before n = "ation". These are "contractions."

At the end of six weeks of excellent teaching and hard practice I could read and write fully contracted Braille. I did both slowly but fluently enough to join the class for all lessons. I then discovered that contractions which meant one thing in English meant something else in another language but this didn't worry me. It was like all the puzzle-solving in Primary School and I enjoyed it.

My classmates asked me why I was repeating Upper Fourth. They had been together for three years since the Third Form so I was rather an interloper. I said: "I'm better at French and things than you but I don't know any German or Braille." They promptly sent me to Coventry for a week. Nobody said a single word to me. They thought I meant "more superior". What I did mean was "further advanced" - but would that have helped? Perhaps I should just have said: I don't know any German or Braille.

My classmates weren't to know the hell I had been through during the past three years, both at school and in the Orphanage. Therefore they didn't know what a mortal wound that sending to Coventry caused me. There I was, beginning a new life. I was free of the Children's Home. I was no longer going to have blackboard problems. I was no longer going to have beatings. I was no longer going to have to listen to little ones suffering. I could start afresh. I actually started by spending a week in silence.

No-one who hasn't been there can possibly know what being sent to Coventry is like. I suppose it is bad enough if the sinner knows the way round. In a new place, where everything is strange, it is hell. Not knowing anything is bad enough but by far the worst is the loneliness, the isolation and the unwantedness. On the third day Miss Cunningham, blind herself, my Braille teacher and our form mistress, took me for a walk. She asked me why no-one was talking to me. I kept my own counsel; said I'd sort it out myself. "Well, I didn't expect you to tell me but if I can help, do ask." she said. I don't know whether Miss Cunningham suggested a truce; whether the girls officially granted me a reprieve; or whether they just got bored with it. Whatever the reason, they started talking to me a few days later.

There was a lot to learn. For one thing, I had never seen a blind person before so I didn't know what to expect or what to do. What I didn't expect was to see them all going up and downstairs or along the corridor as if they could see. In time I learned that "blind" doesn't necessarily mean total blackness. There are hundreds of gradations between that and 20/20 vision. Very soon I found that I had almost the best sight of any of the girls - except in dim light or darkness, when I was worse off than many of them, so I wasn't any use as a partner at night. Even now I haven't learnt to handle the see/no see/see pattern of vision when I go from light/dim/light because my eyes take half an hour to change. One thing I had to learn was not to help blind girls unless they really needed it. Independence was the keyword and I often had to stifle an impulse to lend a hand. One area in which help was needed was in reading people's letters to them. There is an art in reading someone else's letter and I had to learn it. There was always someone who had one to be read just before morning prayers and mostly they were straightforward. The most difficult part of the art though was to read letters containing bad news or matters confidential. Words of sympathy had to be withheld until the bad news had been read but a short warning had to be given first.

Almost the worst thing to learn was playing the piano in public. At morning prayers the hymn was always played by one of the girls. Learning to play the piano was compulsory so most of us had one or two hymns in our repertoire. We could choose the hymn for our birthday and I always hoped that no-one would choose one of mine. The piano was in front of the girls and to the side of the staff so the staff were only a few feet away.

One of my most embarrassing moments is associated with hymn-playing. "Thy Kingdom come, O God" is a hymn with a four-line verse. Each line has six chords. The hymn has five verses. It is the easiest hymn in the book to play and it was mine. The first time it came up I sat at the piano and played the introductory note. Then the first line. After that my mind went blank. My fingers waited for instructions. They didn't get any and the girls finished the verse unaided. I started the second verse. Same thing - and so on for the rest of the hymn. By the end of the fifth verse I was scarlet with embarrassment. I was also frightened. I had done something very wrong. My music teacher - we had two - was furious. I had a music lesson that day and I had to play that wretched hymn over and over again. All the girls had to practise their hymns in their lessons that week, too. I was not at all popular. Four weeks later it was All Saints Day. The hymn, "For All the Saints..." was, again, mine. I was quaking when I sat down. Bong. I played the lead-in note and off we went. Not a note wrong throughout. Whew! After prayers, Miss Wise, the senior music teacher came over to me. "Joan, you played that beautifully, but oh dear! You didn't give us any time to breathe." She laughed and I managed a nervous smile.

A lasting memory of Chorleywood College is the singing. This was no reedy, ragged singing. We were taught to sing properly and we sang everything in harmony. Even Grace before meals was sung and in harmony. Quite often, lazing in our free time, someone would start humming and the rest of us would gradually join in. Within seconds we would be in full voice and full harmony. We would sing if there were only three or four of us.

Music was a great feature of life at school.

O music, come and light my heart's dark places.

It did indeed. Its power to heal was sorely needed in those days. We could ask permission to stay up at bedtime to listen to classical music on the radio and I have a special love of Beethoven's Seventh Symphony because it was the first piece of music I ever stayed up for.

The highlight of our musical world, though, was the Robert Mayer concerts. Robert Mayer was a 19th Century businessman, who founded children's concerts in London and many other cities. The concerts were so popular with us that names had to be drawn out of a hat and we could only go to two concerts each in a term. The outing would start with a coach ride to Central Hall, Westminster. Then there was the Hall itself, packed with children; the excitement of the orchestra tuning up; the instant and total hush when the conductor raised his baton. There was no coughing or chattering. Then the concert itself. Magic.

The crystal set introduced me to another great delight: the Test Match. When they were on we were riveted to the wireless. Those were the days of Len Hutton; Denis Compton; Eric Hollies; Ramadin and Valentine; Norman Yardley. What heroes!

Every Wednesday afternoon we had our Club meetings. I belonged to the Country Dance Club and loved the dances - Thadi, you gander; Water Boatman; Circassian Circle; they were all wonderful. Once a year a Country Dance Summer Festival was held at Welwyn Garden City and we went to it, dressed in bright dirndl skirts and pretty blouses. This was the opening of the doors to real life; it was fairyland for me.

At night I would read books in print to the other girls by torchlight. Books like "The Angry Mountain" by Hammond Innes. If my friends weren't in the same dormitory as me I would go to theirs. Or someone else would come to ours. Sometimes we made too much noise and a member of staff would come; then any visitor would slip down into the bed she was on and hope to avoid detection. We usually did because the staff seldom put the light on.

When I first started breaking rules with the other girls I was afraid. I used to have a dreadful sinking feeling whenever we were caught but gradually I learnt that dire consequences didn't follow; then I began to enjoy the mischief. It was marvellous knowing that we could be naughty without drastic repercussions.

We could keep pets if we wanted to and many of us did; white rats, hamsters, rabbits, guinea-pigs. It was in my first year that I acquired my rabbit which I called Lepis. The rabbit was almost stone-coloured and I tended it with loving care. We took our pets home in the holidays, of course and I took my rabbit back to the Children's Home at Christmas and at Easter. My Lepis was the rabbit I trod on, which was the main reason why I was so upset, why I swore at Sister Penelope, but I got no comfort in my sorrow. I was back to real life.

When I went back to school after the Easter holidays I left Lepis at the Children's Home. Animals were caged at school and I have always hated to see animals cooped up. My rabbit would be happier in the rabbit run at The Haven.

That was also the Easter holiday when I was confronted with my letter to Miss Roslyn; when I was told that I was mentally disturbed. Two crises in three weeks. I couldn't wait to get back to school and away from it all.

My school work in that first year was fine. I got a Certificate for Examination Results at the end of the year. My average mark was 75%. I also got a Certificate for Commended Work. They were given for a good standard of work during the year. What a difference from my last year in Grammar school!

Chorleywood College had an accessible library so I had been able to read the books I was supposed to read and I had done the work I was supposed to do. With only 63 pupils in all, classes were very small so individual attention was possible if we needed it and I was doing well.

The second year started well enough, though I was still trying to make a mother-figure of Miss Roslyn. All my friends had mothers and fathers and my own longings were therefore accentuated; they were much nearer the surface. During the Christmas term I was already writing to my aunt, my mother's sister. My need to know about my mother was uppermost in my mind now and it was beginning to distract me from my work. I wasn't doing quite as well as in the previous year but I was still well within the bounds of acceptability. My Christmas term report wasn't quite as complimentary as the last year's had been and Sister Penelope began to mutter, Sister Annette to sharpen her tongue.

In the Easter term I could stand the strain no longer so I wrote to my aunt and arranged the fateful visit. The exquisite pain and grief of my mother's total rejection of me was almost too hard to bear and I was being torn apart by the knowledge that there was to be no mother in my life. I did tell the girls at school the facts but I never told them about the desolation. The disillusion, the shattering of dreams, the profound depths of suffering inside me was for me alone.

Gym lessons and Greek Flops were replaced by swimming lessons in the summer term. Everyone else swam in Garden Exercise, the replacement for the daily walk. Second swims were not allowed and I was the only one who ever tried it. There would be very few girls in the pool during Garden Exercise - most classes had their swims during lessons - so I could only try it if Miss Freedman, the games mistress, wasn't on pool duty. In my first year at Chorleywood I would slither into the pool hoping that no-one had seen me. When Miss Freedman came to check, which she often did, I would duck-dive. I would swim two lengths underwater. Then I would surface, hoping that the games mistress had gone away. Too often she hadn't and her sandals would be on the edge waiting for me when I came up for air but I enjoyed the fun of trying to get away with it.

In the summer term following the abortive visit to see my mother I tried three lengths underwater. I pushed myself to the limits of breath control to concentrate my mind. It didn't help; the wound was still raw and bleeding. I was still drowning in a sea of wretchedness. I didn't get away with many second swims but I didn't try very hard that year. I wasn't feeling much like playing.

In the classroom my schoolwork was on a slow decline. I tried hard but my enthusiasm and concentration had gone. I was beginning to face downhill again. My end-of-year report and Miss Donellan's letter to Sister Penelope brought school and Children's Home back together with a bang. Sister Penelope was angry and Sister Annette was talking of expulsion.

During the summer holidays Lisa's mother collided with the full force of my misery, anger, fear and frustration. I had learnt that physical abuse and mental cruelty were not the way to hand out punishment. That was when I wrote to Inspector B; when I learned that I wasn't too old to be thrashed and when the Reverend Mother carved me into tiny pieces, scraped them together and sent them back to The Haven.

> While shivering in my shoes
> I strike a careless pose
> And whistle a happy tune
> So no-one will suppose
> I'm afraid.

> (From The King and I)

Ever looking for someone, anyone to praise and encourage me, I tried particularly hard to get Miss Freedman's praise in an area where I was good; Sportex and swimming. It didn't work.

In my third Christmas term I tried even harder. Miss Freedman flatly refused to give me any personal word of commendation. I tried to throw two, even three boundaries in the same game of

Sportex. Two wasn't very usual; three was unheard of. Usually I managed it but sometimes I threw a "minus" instead. A boundary was like kicking into touch in rugby. The further we threw the ball the greater the advantage. To throw less than halfway down the pitch before the ball crossed the line was a "minus" and it could cost quite a few points. When I threw a "minus" I got all the attention I had been looking for from Miss Freedman, attention I could well have done without. I pretended I didn't care. I pretended very hard. I wasn't getting many pats on the back in the classroom either. We had started the run-in to O Levels and I was facing further downhill. Miss Roslyn had left to get married. That was a good thing anyway. She had wanted to get rid of me. I whistled my happy tune.

The Christmas holidays during those Chorleywood years were always reasonably calm for me. There was the odd bonk from a saucepan or a rolling pin but not much else. However, underneath the calm Sister Penelope was getting angrier and Sister Annette was getting more acid as my reports got worse so I kept out of trouble as much as possible. The Christmas holidays were short; about two and a half weeks. Preparation for Christmas, Midnight Mass and Christmas Day took up most of the time. Then there was only about a week before I went back to school.

My schoolwork wasn't too bad during the Easter term that year. I had tried really hard to reach O Level standard. The staff began to make more encouraging noises and I was still whistling. My term report was an improvement. I was coming out of the Slough of Despond and I was reasonably hopeful of passing O Levels - till Sister Annette stopped my whistling. She and I weren't getting on at all well together by then. Explosions were frequent and violent. I was incensed when she accused me of not having been to Confession that Easter. I had been comforted and, I thought, strengthened by Brother Bernard, the Merthyr Brother, but Sister Annette had kicked that support from under me. Priests could say what they liked. It didn't change a thing. I was beginning to hate Sister Annette. The angry exchange over my Confession cost me dear.

Shortly after Easter Rosie's brother came to see her. He smoked and asked Sister Annette if he could smoke in the Home. "Of course," she said. "Please do. I love the smell of cigarettes." So he smoked.

That evening, when he had left, Sister Annette was vitriolic about it. I pointed out that she herself had given him permission. "Don't you be so rude," she said crossly, "and don't answer back." I went up to the playroom out of her way. Rosie was up in the playroom. "What's Sister Annette saying about my brother?" she wanted to know. "Leave it" I urged. "Take it from whence it comes. She's not worth it" but Rosie had to know so I told her. We released some of our dammed up feelings by taking Sister Annette to pieces. Suddenly the door flew open and there she stood. She was a tall woman and she was seething. "Go to bed." she snapped at Rosie. Rosie went at speed. I forestalled Sister Annette by saying rudely: "If you heard what we were saying it serves you right for listening at doors." At that Sister Annette was more furious than I thought she could be. Usually she was controlled and malicious. This time she was like a burst steam pipe. "It's a pity you ever have to come back here during the holidays." she hissed. "You cause nothing but trouble when you're here. You are discontented yourself and you upset all the other girls." I took refuge in fury. "Do you think I would come back to this bloody place if I had anywhere else to go?" but the door slammed before I had finished.

Loppy, one of the three dogs, had been lying on the window-seat. He had got up and was growling. He was a cross between an English collie and a German shepherd and he looked on himself as *my* dog. He was the reason why Sister Penelope whipped me in the Parlour or up in my bedroom. Loppy would have gone for her and Sister Penelope knew it. She was a farmer's daughter. That was probably also part of the reason why Sister Annette left me so quickly. I put my arms round Loppy and cried into his fur. I wasn't discontented. I was lonely and distressed and I was desperately unhappy but, as I had with Sister Annette, I hid it under prickles and nonchalance. I still had over two years of it and it seemed like eternity. Sister Annette and I didn't speak to each other for three days.

I went back to school soon afterwards, weary and disheartened. It was O Level time but I didn't care. I made an effort in class and did my homework, all to no avail. My heart wasn't in it. Nothing really mattered. The staff, one by one, went to Miss Donellan and told her that if I didn't pull myself together I wouldn't pass O Levels. Miss Donellan called me to her office and told me what the staff had said. She warned me that I wouldn't get O Levels at the rate I was going. I stared blankly at her. None of the staff had said anything to me. Miss Bernice, the Maths teacher, was the only one who did. She was genuinely worried for me and she asked me what the trouble was. "Nothing." I said briefly. "It would be different if you hadn't done the work," Miss Bernice went on; "But look at it. All neatly laid out and nothing right. I'll have to tell Miss Donellan..."

How could she have known what that did to me. I was sick to death of all the telling and the writing, the reporting and the warning. I exploded. "Well, go on then. You're the only one that hasn't." Poor Miss Bernice, so gentle and kind hearted. Like an angry wasp I stung her.

Miss Donellan sent for me again. This time she questioned me more closely. Boyfriend? Whatever could that have to with it? Ours was a single-sex school and no boys were ever invited. I was not allowed out in the Children's Home, even at sixteen. Chance would be a fine thing. "No, I haven't." I answered with surprise. "Well, are you in trouble here?" "No." "At home?" "No, I'm not." I said sharply. Home? Pah! "Well, something must be worrying you." Is it this? Is it that? This? That? On and on till I gave in. "All right! I had some trouble in the holidays. But you can't do anything about it. Nobody can." I was exhausted. "I'll have to write ..." I could have screamed. "...to Sister Penelope because if you don't pull your socks up you're not going to pass your exams." I left the office, exasperated at yet another letter to Sister Penelope. I expected Sister Penelope to write but she didn't. My passport to freedom was getting more and more tatty. With a monumental effort I pulled myself out of the quagmire and faced O Levels. I felt a little happier than I had expected to feel when the exams were finished.

That same term I was caught in one of the girls' beds. We must have been too vociferous in our excitement over the current book for suddenly the door opened and this time the light did go on. We had heard the footsteps so I had just had time to dive under the bedclothes, lying flat in the hope of avoiding detection. It was Miss Donellan and she had obviously seen me. Partially sighted people don't realise how much normally sighted people can see at a distance. Miss Donellan pulled back the bedclothes, gave me a real dressing-down for breaking rules and sent me back to my own dormitory. I left the book I had been reading in the bed I had been in so Miss Donellan hadn't found it.

At half-term Sister Cecily came to see me. She was stationed in one of the Convent's Branch Houses in London. She didn't seem very happy to be visiting me and she had difficulty in keeping up a conversation. I wasn't very pleased either. I had had to turn down a school friend's invitation because of Sister Cecily's visit and we didn't even leave the school. Sister Cecily wandered off fairly early and I hoped Sister Penelope wasn't going to do that very often. She had ruined half-term for me.

Shortly after I returned to The Haven at the end of term, Sister Penelope sent for me. "Miss Donellan says you had trouble in the Easter holidays. She doesn't think you'll pass O Levels. What was the trouble?" What was the point? It wouldn't make any difference. Anyway, in cold blood it lost the power of its wounding. Here we go. This, that? This, that? Wearing, wearing. I told her.

"Do you think I want to come back here in the holidays? I don't want to come any more than you want me but what choice do I have?"

Sister Penelope told me not to worry about such things. Sister Annette probably hadn't meant it. "I've got something far more serious to talk to you about." More serious than tearing me to pieces? Sister Penelope hummed and ha'd. What was the matter with her, I wondered. She didn't usually have any hesitation in slamming into us. "Miss Donellan tells me you've been getting into bed with other girls." Sister Penelope paused. "That's not a very nice thing to do ..." I silently annihilated Miss Donellan. She had ticked me off good and proper at the time for breaking the rules and that should have been that. It usually was. "What's wrong with that?" I asked in surprise. "We all do." Sister Penelope nearly had a heart attack. "Girls of your age shouldn't get into each other's beds. You're too old for that sort of thing. Don't let me hear of it happening again." I was sent away.

What the hell was she talking about? Why were we too old to

get into each other's beds? How else would we keep warm? Why did Sister Penelope make me feel I was doing something wrong? Why was she so embarrassed about it? Anger rising. And why hadn't Miss Donellan told me she was going to tell Sister Penelope? She usually did. What a sneaky thing to do. If it was that bad why hadn't Miss Donellan had Mary and me in the office and told us herself? I found out later that she hadn't told Mary's parents and I was absolutely livid at being singled out. I suppose Miss Donellan thought she stood in loco parentis for me. If she did, I could well have done without such solicitude. It got me into a steady stream of hot water - far more than any of the other girls.

At the same time as this I was looking after Pudding and trying to get through to her and Sister Annette was continually needling me acidly about the probable O Level results. I had wasted all my opportunities etc. etc. When the letter came she sniffed significantly. It was probably to tell me I had failed. Heart in my mouth I opened the letter. Both Sisters were in the kitchen. Both were watching me. I had achieved three Credits, a Distinction in German and a failure in mathematics. As the staff had expected me to fail German they must have been even more flabbergasted than I was. I passed mathematics at the resit. Oh boy! Even Sister Annette couldn't sniff away three credits and a distinction. I went back to school much happier. I had a pretty good O Level result and there was Pudding. She would be waiting for me at The Haven at Christmas.

At the beginning of each year we chose our games captain. In this first year of A Levels the team chose me and Miss Freedman was not at all pleased. She remembered too vividly my increasing striving for personal glory. I had been trying as late as the previous winter. All Miss Freedman didn't know was why. By the time I was games captain I had given up trying but she didn't know that. Also, being a member of a team is one thing. Being captain of it is quite another. I had been in the school team since I had been at Chorleywood and for three years I had tried to win Miss Freedman's favour. For three years I had failed. Now that I was captain I was going to lead our team to victory - we played against a few schools who had learnt the game. I would put everything I'd got into being a good captain and Miss Freedman could go hang.

The best position for me was No. 3 runner. As No. 3 I almost always got three throws. If going for a boundary I could pause just long enough to let two or three runners already on track pass a basket. (The basket had a wooden tapper on it to guide the blind girls.) They then walked to the basket at the other end of the pitch for extra points. Occasionally it wasn't in our interests to have a boundary, or the wind was wrong. Then I dropped the ball at one of my fielder's feet. Throwing a boundary involved so many technicalities: wind direction and force; height of the ball in the air to delay its crossing the line; where the runners were on the track. It was a learned skill and it was exciting. I could use it even more skilfully now that I was no longer playing for myself. At the end of the year I went to talk to Miss Freedman. She agreed that she hadn't wanted me to be captain at the beginning of the year but she had noticed a change in my attitude that year and she was pleased. She didn't know why that was either and I didn't tell her.

Once we reached Lower VI we were automatically prefects. I wasn't. I was only a sub-prefect. Miss Donellan told me that I wasn't yet ready to be a full prefect. It was embarrassing but I was used to being worthless and undeserving. What else could I expect? Then the girls elected me games captain and that helped me a lot. My schoolwork was fine that Christmas term.

I went back to The Haven with anticipation. Pudding would be there and I could look after her. Pudding was not there; she was dead. The sense of theft was unimaginable and when Sister Annette caught me crying and called me sloppy, it was the absolute extreme in human cruelty.

I struggled through the Easter term nursing my grief. I was trying to cope with A Level demands but not very successfully. There was nothing that counted, no-one who cared and there was nowhere to hide. I never had time to recover from one psychological blow before I was flattened by another.

Neither the Economic History nor French teachers were pushers; Miss Ellen, the Latin teacher, was. I had very few resources left; I was almost drained so I directed what little was left to where demand was greatest. The hardest thing was to keep whistling.

In the Easter holidays "trial by bantam cock" was common. It was, by then, just another way of chastising little children. I had felt their terror but the rolling pin crashing onto my shoulder had taught me to keep my mouth shut so from then on I suffered their torment in silence.

Work in the summer term was no easier. I struggled again, and once again I gave Latin my ever-dwindling ability to cope.

Life did have its lighter moments - like the Welwyn Garden Country Dance Festival. That was a colourful, lively, exciting day and it brightened me up just a smidgin. There was also the outdoor theatre. In the summer every year we presented a play at half-term for parents and visitors. We acted it in the shade of one of the huge cedars. The setting was magnificent. That year the drama was the Selfish Giant and I was cast as the North Wind. I had skewers and small knitting needles attached to my grey chequered costume and I had to dance about being very fierce and very spiky. Most appropriate.

O, music come and light my heart's dark places; ...
Arouse to life my spirit's inmost ear ...

Beethoven and Mozart and the beauty of Chorleywood supported me that term. The school building was of sandstone and it glowed golden in the evening light. The cedars stood in majestic splendour, their spicy fragrance intoxicating in the warmth of the sun and the scent of roses blending with the cedars was a delight. Walking in the grounds in the cool of the evening was balm to a troubled soul; the peace was soothing. One more year. Four more holidays at The Haven. Could I stand another year? I went on whistling - at least at school. At The Haven in the summer holidays I wasn't whistling at all. I came within an ace of killing Sister Penelope.

The last year at school started and I went into it with a sense of fatalistic relief. I was facing the possibility that I might fail A Levels. Sister Annette was right. I wasn't doing nearly as well as I should be. Her trouble was that she had a mental block over the reasons. Her unending denigration was one of them.

It was a few weeks after the beginning of that term that I was sent to the priest and my visits to him were my life-jacket. There was a lot of reading to do for Economic History that year and Miss Ellen wouldn't let me skimp Latin, so French, once my favourite subject, almost went by the board. Even with the priest's help I was fast nearing the end of the road, though I don't think anyone knew; it was all shut tight away from view.

After the summer of 1953 Sister Penelope left me alone. She had looked into the waters of the River Styx.. No more rolling pins slammed on to my shoulder. No more saucepans gave me headaches but Sister Annette had one last go at wrecking my life. We were almost always at daggers drawn.

In the Easter holidays we had a Visitor, a Charitable Lady. I was making coffee for her and Sister Annette and they were sitting in the kitchen, watching. The Visitor asked: "Isn't she a bit old to be here? You don't usually keep them that long, do you?"

Does he take sugar? I cut in on Sister Annette. "Yes, *she* is. *She* is still at school." Poor Visitor. She had no idea. "Don't speak to visitors like that." Sister Annette snapped at me. Then, turning back to the Visitor: "Look at her. Great lump of a thing. Still at school and thinking of going to university, if you please." If Sister Annette had her way I wouldn't even make it to A Levels. "She ought to be out earning her living. Not expecting us to keep her all her life." If Sister Annette thought that the Visitor was protection, she soon found she was wrong. Anger was a way of life for me in The Haven by then and I lashed out: "You don't keep me; The L.E.A. does - even my non-uniform clothes and pocket money. It doesn't cost you a penny, so there!" "And who do you think keeps you in the holidays, Madam?" asked Sister Annette acidly. I was choked. "With all the hard work I do, I reckon I more than earn my keep." I retorted and stalked out. The Visitor was appalled. "Is she often as rude as that?" "I've never heard anything like it." said Sister Annette. She sounded rather at a loss.

So they didn't even want me to go to university. Far from being pleased about it they were exasperated. They thought university was a waste of time. It wouldn't be their fault if I got there. They'd done their level best to ruin my chances all along. If I got A Levels it would be out of sheer pig-headedness; my schoolwork hadn't been good enough to deserve it.

I scraped through A Levels, though I did quite well in Latin. Miss Ellen had dragged me there and I had made it. I was too near to total collapse to have done it off my own bat. The other two teachers hadn't tugged me along and I had only just got there.

We had all had to take Religious Knowledge at O Levels at the same time as A Levels and I failed it. Sister Annette rose to her full, self-righteous height. "Failed Religious Knowledge. Cared for all your life in a Christian household and you failed Religious Knowledge. I told you you would come to a bad end." What did she expect? In such a Christian household as The Haven I was bound to fail. The only Christian who had ever taught me anything of real worth was Father Michael.

We used to sing a hymn in church:

> There were ninety and nine that safely lay
> In the shelter of the fold;
> But one was out on the hills away,
> Far off from the gates of gold;
> Away on the mountains wild and bare
> Away from the Tender Shepherd's care.

In the third verse are the lines:

> Out in the desert He heard its cry,
> Sick and helpless and ready to die...

That was another of those fraudulent hymns. God wouldn't have heard us orphans if we'd used a ghetto blaster.

Father Michael, that enlightened priest, had heard my silent plea and had done what he could. He didn't bring me back to the fold, like the sheep in the hymn. It was far too late for that. He couldn't wipe away the seventeen and half years of suffering. The damage was far too extensive and far too deep. That took 26 years and another quite different but equally remarkable person. What Father Michael did do was to give me a brief glimpse of the sky above the rubble. There was a way out of it if I could only find it.

I said nothing to Sister Annette. I might have had the last word in the Visitor episode but Sister Annette had the last word with my destiny. She had undermined my confidence about going to university. I would be a nurse instead.

On August 6th 1954 the forbidding door of The Haven closed behind me for the last time. I was free. I could start to live a normal life; to try and find that release from the rubble which Father Michael had hinted was there. I was nineteen years old.

ENTR'ACTE:

KINDLIER SOULS

"were all thy children kind and natural."
Shakespeare; King Henry V, II Chorus 16

Deep inside me is a still, silent pool;
Its surface is unruffled by the world outside;
It is guarded by a quickset hedge of thorns
To keep at bay the uncaring intruder.
No-one may plant flowers on its banks
Lest, planting them, he cease to tend them
And they wither and die
Leaving the place more desolate than before.

Edwards, P.J. 1959
The Heart of a Child in Care, in:
Women in Poetry, 1993, p.189
Ed.Hannan, Veronica,
Publishers, Poetry Now, Peterborough

Chapter 1

A Different Life

"....spite of fears ...remember not the past."
Cardinal Newman; Pillar of Cloud.

On a fine, sunny day I took the train to Paddington. I had a small suitcase containing my worldly possessions. It was no trouble to carry it; there wasn't a lot in it. Uniform would be provided when I got to Preliminary Training School (PTS) like it had been at Chorleywood College. I changed to the Underground and went to Mill Hill. There I joined twenty-nine other girls at the Charing Cross Group PTS for nurses. My new life had begun.

It had been less difficult than I had expected to get a place in a School of Nursing. I had persuaded Miss Donellan that I really did want to be a nurse, so she had arranged three interviews. The first two matrons didn't want to know. The third, Miss Martin, of Harrow Hospital in Middlesex, was much more helpful. First she checked that I wasn't likely to throw a wobbly over a sudden revelation of family history. Then she said she would give me a chance on two conditions. The first was that I should see the Group's senior eye specialist. The second was that if I put any patient in the slightest danger I would be out on my ear. I agreed.

The eye specialist thought that I would be all right; I wasn't likely to put a patient at risk. He had asked me to read what it said on a postage stamp. I read "Harrison" on the white border because I thought that that was what he wanted. The eye specialist was amazed. He looked at the border through a magnifying glass. "So it does," said he. "You might not be able to see very far but you have microscopic vision close to."

113

Once my training began I did my best to hide the fact that I couldn't see very well. If people are expecting trouble or looking for it they usually find it. Also, Sister Thelma's long disdain and irritation over my poor sight and its consequences had left their mark. I still had a lurking fear and shame among sighted people though, strangely, at Chorleywood it had been different. Extreme short-sightedness isn't easy to hide but fellow students were always ready to help if I would let them. Gradually I learnt to compensate. I developed a range of tactics to cope in dim light or the dark, just like the girls at school had. I counted the number of stairs on dark staircases, along corridors and so on. Motivation is all. I learnt all the things I should have learnt at Chorleywood.

I didn't talk about the Children's Home. I wanted to put it all behind me but it was soon common knowledge. I suppose that the Sisters had been told and, mysteriously, that kind of knowledge soon spreads, anyway. People would say to me: "People would never guess you're from a Children's Home, you know. You're too normal." What did they expect an orphan to be like? It just shows what wearing a cheerful smile can do.

PTS is where nurses learn basic knowledge and procedures so that when they go to the wards they aren't completely useless. We learnt anatomy and physiology (how the body works); basic nursing techniques; hygiene and first aid. We learnt how to give injections; how to bath a patient in bed; how to prepare a patient for the operating theatre and so on.

I enjoyed that period of study, cosily in classroom or practical room. We had a female dummy for learning practical procedures and models of organs for learning anatomy. We built up a skeleton from a heap of bones; we took an eye to pieces; we put organs into their right place in the body. Problem-solving. It was great fun. We also skated over the male reproductive system but we had no models. What we did learn about it was taught by a rather bashful Sister Tutor and she certainly didn't prepare us for reality. What she did do was to enhance my belief that there was something "not quite nice" about men. This view I had of the opposite sex, built up over so many years of disparagement, warnings and threats by the Sisters of Mercy, was to play a major part in my life for years to come. Never having had any close contact with fathers, uncles, brothers or "friends of the family", I had no means of knowing that it wasn't necessarily true.

I tried for perfection in all aspects of the study and practice. Detention at school and re-doing jobs in the Children's Home were still very fresh in my mind. I think I'm a perfectionist by nature but in those days I wouldn't have known the difference. After three months we had examinations, both theoretical and practical. I got high marks in both and was among the top five. I even took the prize in Hygiene and First Aid. At least I had started well.

Charing Cross Group was made up of several hospitals and at the end of PTS most students went to Charing Cross Hospital itself, a London Teaching Hospital. Three of us went to Harrow. This was a small hospital, with 120 beds, so its scope was limited. There was no head or chest surgery or Maternity Unit, for example, though all could be dealt with as emergency.

My first ward was Male Surgical. At 7.30 a.m., on November 10th 1954 I went into the ward office in fear and trembling. The morning started with the report from the night nurse in charge. "Collapsed...Drip...doctor called...slept for long periods...Emergency admitted..." Such a lot went on during the night. My head was whirling at the end. I had understood almost nothing.

At the desk sat a tall, blonde woman in mid-blue - Sister Collier, the Sister of the ward. She was an excellent Sister, with a businesslike, rolled-up-sleeves, teach-by-example approach. She either taught or supervised new students personally or delegated all but the basics to the Senior Staff-Nurse. Sister stood no nonsense but she was just and fair. It was a real pleasure to have her as a teacher.

On that first morning she introduced me to the rest of the staff and put me in the care of a senior student, Nurse Ruffle. We worked together and she was very considerate to me. She was neither bossy nor superior as many students were. We bed-bathed patients who were confined to bed and treated their pressure areas. These are the areas where prolonged pressure can cause an agonising sore - the lower end of spine, the heels and the elbows. Massaging these areas will usually prevent such sores.

During those three months on Men's Surgical I learned to give injections and enemas; change surgical dressings and shorten drainage tubes; take out stitches, prepare patients for operation and so on. I was comfortable with it all - bar one thing. We had to shave patients before operation. An arm or leg was no problem. Even the chest and abdomen was all right but to shave the genitals was quite frightful. I expect all students were embarrassed by it but for me it was panic-stations. We hadn't even been allowed to show our "vulgar knees" in The Haven and talking to a boy had been tantamount to prostitution. Now here I was, doing the most intimate things to men and it was almost impossible to cope with it. My schooling in prudery and my short sight turned it into a nightmare. I was terrified of cutting a patient and my sight would be blamed, - the fatal mistake. Nothing else on that ward gave me such jitters. Except for one incident.

One morning I was asked to give a patient his pre-operation injection. I should have had a staff-nurse with me but we were short-staffed. 'Flu was carrying off the staff in droves. I gave the patient the injection in his arm. I had by this time, given dozens and it was perfectly simple. I withdrew the needle - and my heart dropped like a stone into my boots. The patient had gone a dirty grey colour and was clearly in deep shock. Oh, Lord! What had I done? This had never happened before and there hadn't been anything odd about the injection. I wanted to run away. Let someone else find him...

I pressed the patient's panic-button long and hard. Sister and a staff-nurse arrived at the same time. With calm efficiency they turned the patient on his side and sent for the doctor. There was a general air of emergency and fear for life. I was sent to the ward as soon as I had told them what had happened. Somehow I had endangered that patient's life. He was very ill as it was and I had made him much worse. Matron's warning came back in full force, I had been able to see perfectly well but the patient was still at death's door. With the fatalism I had learnt in The Haven I awaited the summons and dismissal. On tenterhooks I struggled through the day as best I could. No-one said anything amiss to me and all seemed normal but I was glad we were short-staffed. We were all working like Trojans and our off-duty was either changed or cut so I had little time to brood.

The patient's condition improved during the day, much to my relief. That wouldn't save me though. The operation was really essential to save the patient's life but he wasn't well enough to go to the theatre until after the night staff came on. In the morning report we were told that the patient had again gone into shock after another pre-operation injection. He was either sensitive to the drug or he was just too ill.

It was such a weight off my mind to know that I hadn't harmed him. I was also grateful beyond measure that I wasn't going to have to go. Not this time but I was aware then how delicately the Sword of Damocles hung over my head. There it stayed throughout the thirteen years of my nursing life.

Ward followed ward and life got easier as knowledge and experience grew. Some procedures were beyond me - like taking out the tiny stitches used in plastic surgery - but I usually managed to avoid doing these. If I couldn't I mentally shut my eyes and crossed my fingers.

Night duty was by far the worst test. As students we did three months each year. My spell always came up during the hours of greatest light - mid-April to mid-July. I'm sure Miss Martin, the Matron, arranged it like that intentionally. It was a great help to me because it was light before patients were awake and they were tucked down before it was really dark. As it happened my first night duty was on the medical ward. There were almost no emergencies and the junior nurse skivvied outside the ward all night. We were expected to stand to attention at the door when the Night Sister came to do her rounds. Then the junior had to be neither seen nor heard.

On night duty I always learnt the layout of the ward, how many steps from here to there and which patient was in which bed. I learnt to assess a patient's condition by his or her breathing and how to find a wrist by touch to take a pulse. Anything else needed the patient's bed-light anyway. Somehow I got through without mishap.

In our second and third years we did a turn on the Accident and Emergency (A&E) and Operating Theatre departments. Both were fine because there was always plenty of light, though I preferred the theatre to A&E because I had no responsibility for assessing a patient's condition; that was the business of the anaesthetist and surgeon. The actual work was a mixture of high drama and boredom with a lot of great interest in between. Often there were moments of sudden crisis during an operation but as a student I had no responsibility for these either. They were handled by the Sister or Staff Nurse in charge. I just did as I was told and learnt as I went. I learnt particularly well because I wanted to work in Theatre when I qualified. I would have all the light I needed and therefore I would be able to see clearly what I was doing; there would be no fear of making the wrong decision regarding the patient's condition because that wouldn't be my responsibility; also, there would be no three-month spell of night-duty as there was for ward staff because we were "on call" about twice a week and we weren't always called out.

In 1957, after three years' hard training, I passed the exams. I was a State Registered Nurse. On the day of the results, if we had passed, we always went individually to Miss Martin to get our "black belts" - the mark of the Staff Nurse - and our hospital badge.

I said a heartfelt "thank you" to Miss Martin for having given me a chance. Half-mocking as usual, the Matron laughed. "Thank *you* for having *us*. Think what we'd have missed if you'd gone somewhere else." That was her way of brushing aside her own trust and generosity. "I shall write to Miss Donellan...." for the first time in my life those words held no threat. "...and tell her you're a credit to both us and her." At last someone was really pleased with my success. It was music to my unaccustomed ear. As Miss Martin pinned my belt on I told her I wanted to work in Theatre and a month later I joined the Theatre staff.

As a student nurse I had "scrubbed" for small operations, like removing a cyst or an appendix. As a Staff Nurse I would scrub for major surgery and for the surgeons - not just for the Registrar. A Registrar is a consultant-in-training. "Scrubbing" is washing hands and arms thoroughly, putting on a sterile gown and gloves and giving the surgeon whatever he needs to do his job and generally managing the Theatre staff during the operation.

For two and a half years I worked happily in Theatres. I had no hassles with being "on call" - being called out for an emergency.

The light in theatre always had to be bright and clear. The only difficulty was having to walk along a short but very dimly lit lane to the hospital but a friend taught me self-defence and my hearing is acute, which also helped. Knowing what to do is at least three quarters of the battle. Woe betide anyone who wanted to play the fool. I would have struck first and asked questions afterwards. Young doctors are notorious for playing practical jokes and, as they dated nurses, they were often about when I was called out.

As the third year in the Theatre passed I realised that if I wanted to make that my career I would have to do midwifery training so, in May, 1960, I went to the Royal Maternity Hospital in Belfast. I went without worrying because Miss Martin had said there would always be a place for me at Harrow Hospital. I wondered how much of a hindrance my short sight would be in midwifery. In fact it hardly mattered at all so I had no cause for alarm. I learnt how to deliver babies in hospital and in the home. I learnt how to recognise and deal with emergencies and complications before, during and after birth. At the same time I learnt that God didn't care much for women any more than He did for orphans.

Most of my colleagues were Roman Catholics and they believed steadfastly in God's Will. Whatever happened to us or the world was for a Divine Reason. If a longed-for pregnancy ended in death, it was hard - but God had a Plan. If a young couple gazed down forlornly on a deformed baby, it was a great shame - but God knew what He was doing. If a mother of eight scowled at her healthy ninth, oh dear! She shouldn't. She was blessed by God.

Most babies were hale and hearty and their parents loved them dearly. Their love and tenderness gladdened the heart. However, the Royal Maternity Hospital in Belfast dealt with all abnormal pregnancies in Northern Ireland so my view of childbirth was distorted. I thought that far more pregnancies went wrong than actually did. God's "Boundless Mercy" seemed to be sadly lacking, just as it had been in the Orphanage. The women also believed that He was doing His Best for them but if He were, He seemed very incompetent to me. Sometimes a mother would cry aloud: "Why has God done this to me?" and her sorrow was heart-rending. I couldn't tell her that there was no God. I couldn't explain about the way we were made, how we lived or what illnesses we had had. She wouldn't have believed me. If I had still believed in God I would have got rid of Him then. He was still as sadistic as in my childhood. Why did Man create such a monster? When I had shown God and the Devil the door I hadn't replaced them with anything. Now, in midwifery, I had "seen the light". Our lives were controlled by nurture, chance, opportunity and environment; all the human things which shape us from childhood. Our code of morality was our own affair. No Supreme Tyrant told us what to do. Sometimes I had moments of deep peace and serenity, like the peace which had come with the light from the west window at Evensong.

After a year of childbirth and soul-searching I went back to Harrow Hospital. I was a State Certified Midwife. I wanted nothing more than to go back there and work happily ever after.

I loved every aspect of nursing. I had a respected role and I could hide behind the uniform to some extent though very early on, a few of the marks of my past became clearly evident. Some were crippling; some were more helpful: I was persevering to the point of pig-headedness and that was to stand me in good stead; I could be led almost anywhere but a single push and I was immovable; that wasn't so useful. In those days nursing was hierarchical, if not dictatorial, and, as in The Haven, I strongly resented the authoritarianism, especially as I thought I had left all that behind. The latter is still with me but I grew out of some consequences fairly quickly.

When I started nursing I had great difficulty in knowing right from wrong; not morally but in practical things. I had had no time to lose my conviction that "not knowing" was a failing so if I didn't know how to do something, I didn't ask. I just muddled along - unless it was a serious matter. Then I would have to ask, sure though I was that it would diminish me in other people's eyes. Gradually, I noticed that other nurses were asking "how, what, where, when, why?" and no-one seemed to blame them for not knowing. On the other hand people were beginning to get exasperated with me. "Why didn't you ask?" they would say, sometimes crossly. "You only had to ask. I would have told you." Tentatively at first, then more boldly, I started asking too. It helped so much.

One defence mechanism, which took a bit longer to leave behind, occasionally caused me acute embarrassment. One instance lives forever in my memory because it came out into the open. Sister Collier was demonstrating a technique which a Staff Nurse was to teach me. She raised her arm sharply above her head and instinctively, I threw my arms over my head and ducked away. Sister Collier was flabbergasted. "Whatever's the matter with you, Nurse? You looked as if you thought I was going to hit you." How could I tell her that that was exactly what I had thought? I don't often blush but on that occasion I was crimson to the roots of my hair. I said nothing but Sister Collier was very careful not to move quickly again. She could always walk about in other people's shoes. Less obvious was my fear of having people behind me. I always kept them in front if possible. Sometimes someone would say: "Oh, for goodness sake, Joan, get a move on." It was some time before I lost my fear of the boot.

There were two deep-seated problems, however, which made all the others seem minor by comparison. One was my absolute inability to accept any form of criticism. The other was an almost pathological anxiety about making decisions.

Criticism is inextricably part of learning and of life but I saw it only as a threat. I believed that liking and approval were measured on a points system and that points were deducted for every blunder and mistake I made; for every less likeable facet of my nature I showed; for every hurt I inflicted. I was certain that, as my points quota was reduced, my image was gradually wiped out, even if people started by liking me. I didn't measure people like that but I thought they were all better than me. I hadn't lost my aggressiveness and hostility whenever I felt threatened and at the slightest hint of disapproval I would man the guns. I had an enormous inferiority complex and I had to be successful to show people that I was all right really. Thus my reports also said: "Must learn to accept criticism. Must learn to take correction with more grace. Resents any form of criticism." and so on. Often when I was corrected I tried to justify myself, especially when I didn't want to lose the approval of someone whose good opinion I valued. I tried to stifle my self-justification when I saw that it didn't go down very well but it didn't always work.

It was soon after I began working on the wards that I became aware of my fear of making decisions. On the wards I was afraid of causing harm to a patient; both on and off the wards I was scared of getting into trouble. Not that I never made decisions; I had to, especially once I became a third year student nurse, in charge of Women's Surgical Ward during the last night duty of my training. It was just that, having made the decision, I worried and pummelled at it, looking for the flaw which I knew must be there.

So much more, however, never showed at all. Some people, when they knew I was from a Children's Home, would say blithely: "You never miss what you've never had." Could they honestly believe that? Most people seemed to think that if there were no outward signs, there was no harm done but they couldn't see the wounds, the turmoil, the longing within. I wasn't withdrawn - on the surface. I wasn't bitter; I wasn't morose. I was quiet and composed, companionable and cheerful but I knew what I was missing, all right. I hadn't left that behind in the Children's Home.

Chapter 2

Leisure Time

"...play on; give me excess of it..."
Shakespeare: Twelfth Night,   1,I

In PTS we were free every evening but I had no idea how to use this freedom. For one thing I wasn't used to having leisure time as such and for another, I didn't know what there was to do. Luckily, we were all new together. We were learning each other and the neighbourhood and we would go out in groups when we had finished writing up our notes for the day. Weekends were the most difficult. Many of the girls went home or to friends on Friday evening but I stayed at the hostel with the rest. "The rest" were different most weekends.

There were two dogs at the hostel, one a huge Samoyed called Wendy. She and I took to each other straightaway and I used to brush her, bath her, walk her. She was always gleaming white and that gave me a real sense of achievement and pleasure. Thus I occupied my weekends and hid my loneliness.

As we students got to know each other we settled into friendships. The girl who had the bed next to me in the dormitory was called June Knight. We were very good friends during our training but when she left for New Zealand after qualification I lost touch. It was "out of sight, out of mind" for me in those early years.

I needed to know that people wanted me to be with them so even if one of the girls I didn't particularly like suggested a film I went; or a coffee house I went. Coffee-housing then was as discos are today - mainly for the young. We would go to two or three in one evening - rather like a teetotal pub crawl. Coffee houses served the new expresso coffee and luscious cakes - which I could never afford. I sometimes borrowed £1 off Miss Russell to keep my end up and to hide my poverty. All the others seemed to have enough money but perhaps some of them borrowed, like I did. A nurse's pay never went very far. I never said: "I'd rather do so-and-so." Or "What about...?" I was just glad to be with someone. I was always afraid that if I proposed something, whoever I was with wouldn't want to do it and would leave me on my own. My life was still run for me by others but in a much nicer way. The spin-off was that I didn't have to make decisions.

Once we started at the hospital we were supposed to study in the evenings but we seldom did, except when exams were looming. We could stay out until 11 pm but we had to have a pass if we wanted to be later.

At first I did nothing. I just sat in my room and read a book. I wasn't used to doing things by myself and, being November, it was too dark to get about in the evenings, anyway. I could see just well enough in the new sodium lighting along the main roads but in minor roads there were only spaced lights. I learned how to cope with them but it took time. I committed kerbs, steps and obstacles to memory in the daylight and walked slowly from lamp to lamp in the dark. This gave me much more leeway and after a while I was ready to go out alone.

One of the two who had started with me at Harrow dropped out after a few weeks. The other one was a Jamaican, Kathleen Barned. She was great fun and we were good friends. She had never seen snow and prayed for some that first winter. We got lots of it and soon the steep hill up to the hospital was very slippery. Kathleen and I, and one or two others, would stand at the kerb and shout to the drivers of the cars; "Don't change gear! We'll push you." They were nearly at the top of the hill by then and usually changed gear for the last little bit. We'd push them over the brow and had enormous fun doing it. One driver lived just at the top and on Christmas Eve invited us in for martinis and mince-pies. I was ever ready for any kind of fun; it was still a great novelty.

When Kathleen and I had the same off-duty we would sometimes go out somewhere - a film, a coffee-house. If we couldn't afford it or the weather was bad we watched television. In the sitting-room, where there were large, cushioned arm-chairs and sofas, I would curl up, as contented as any cat. What luxury!

In the 1950s we worked an 8-hour day, excluding meal times. If we were lucky we got two evenings off in a week but the highlight of the week was our half-day and day off. Occasionally, we would be asked to change these at a moments notice or we could lose our evening off altogether. Any arrangements we made were therefore "subject to availability."

Since Harrow Hospital was small, everyone knew everybody else and I soon got to know several fellow-students. A few of us were bound to be off at the same time and we would all - or some - go out together. I was always ready for the cinema; always eager to go to Westerns, with the immortal John Wayne, or films like Lawrence of Arabia - the sort of films that the girls had talked about at Grammar School. It was years before I took the cinema for granted.

The theatre was even more exciting. Hospitals used to get free tickets to shows or plays and they were soon snapped up. "Salad Days", "Oklahoma", "At The Drop of a Hat," "Murder in the Cathedral" - I saw them all and loved the excitement of it all. The hush as the lights dimmed and the curtain went up or the projector started to roll. Wonderland. We saw far more with the special tickets than we could ever have afforded.

The jewel in the crown were the concerts at the Royal Albert Hall. These were out of my financial range but I could go free on occasion. The Children's Ward Sister had a friend called Cyril. I can't remember his other name. Cyril was an elderly man and he was blind. He had a season ticket for the Albert Hall and anyone could go free as his escort. Many of the nurses were a bit hesitant about escorting a blind person but it was second nature to me with my Chorleywood experience. Cyril was an interesting and serene person and he was good company. It was no trouble to go with him and the concerts were marvellous.

Art thou troubled?
Music will calm thee...

It still played a large part in my life. The concerts helped enormously in the more difficult areas.

I learnt to skate. I went to Finchley Road baths to swim. I bought a second-hand man's bicycle. They are much steadier for long cycle rides. I cycled over to Chorleywood once when I went to see Mrs Heymann and the ride through the Hertfordshire countryside was magnificent. In the 1950s there was very little traffic on the road, compared with today, so I was able to do this in spite of my short sight. Even so, I had to take great care and by the mid-1960s it was out of the question.

In the first summer of my training I had a fortnight's holiday. I didn't want to admit to anybody that I had nowhere to go so I decided to join the children in Bratton Seymour, in Somerset, where The Haven had exchanged with another Home. I cycled all the way there, stopping at Andover overnight.

I was very timid about going into a hotel and I only plucked up the courage when twilight came. I went into the Railway Arms like a cat testing new territory. Bed, breakfast and dinner were cheap enough but the bath cost extra. I was far too unversed and shy to go to the restaurant for supper but I had my bath. It helped to soak away the saddle-soreness of my first long cycle ride. I had a roll and some biscuits left over from my lunch and they and a glass of water were my supper. I had to go to the restaurant for breakfast but it wasn't as bad as I thought it would be. I was used to getting up early and I was by myself for most of the meal. The waitress was a kindly soul and realised that I hadn't a clue. She helped me with ordering and chatted to me for some of the time.

I shopped for lunch in a small grocer's before starting off. Outside the shop was a man's bike and inside was its owner buying his lunch. We chatted over the groceries and found we were going in the same direction. "We could go as far as Wincanton together if you'd like to." said Peter. I liked very much and we set off into the morning freshness of a perfect summer day. We stopped at Stonehenge to have a rest and a drink. I had never seen Stonehenge before and its ancient grandeur was awesome. I could hardly tear myself away.

Peter wanted to see the Wylye Valley and Cley Hill, west of Warminster so we went south west to Wylye and then back in a north easterly direction to Warminster. It wasn't the quickest route from Stonehenge to Wincanton but it wasn't the kind of day for straight routes or heads-down cycling. We ambled along the Wylye Valley via tortuous country lanes, the river coming and going in sun and dappled shade. It was idyllic.

When we reached Warminster Peter suggested that we had a snack before going on to Cley Hill but I didn't want to stop. For one thing I couldn't afford to buy lunch but I didn't tell him that. "Look," said Peter, realising my problem, I think, "I didn't expect to have such pleasant company for so much of the journey. Anyway, I'm hungry and I'd like to give you lunch." I accepted and we had egg and chips in Ted's cafe.

It was a glorious day. Wild flowers abounded and larks soared joyfully, singing their heads off. The odd car bumbled past and cycling lazily through the countryside was a real pleasure. Peter taught me how to hang on to a lorry going uphill - if one was handy when we needed it. We laughed, we chatted, we bowled along in happy fellowship. When Peter left me at Wincanton to go his own way I was genuinely sorry to say goodbye.

"Goodbye," said Peter, "it's been real fun. It's much nicer if you have company." I agreed. It had been one of the happiest, most relaxed days I had ever spent. I went on to Bratton Seymour in a glow of warm feeling.

Mercifully, I had only arranged to be in Bratton for a few days. I spent three days in the Nurses' Hostel before and after the trip. With the four days' travelling, I kept the visit to four days. I had half-thought it would all be different. I had vowed never to return to The Haven itself - and I never did. On holiday though? Less fraught? Less harsh? I should have known better. It never had been. The only difference was that, after a year away from it all, my defences against The Haven were down. The dogs were at Bratton Seymour; so, too, were their leashes. They didn't have a holiday. The cuffs, the blows, the kicks, the whippings, the brutality, the lash of the tongue - they were all still there but not for me. I was outside it all now. There was a baby in a pram and if we weren't out on a picnic I took it for walks - with the dogs. Perhaps someone didn't get a whipping because I had the leashes with me. What a puny effort.

I was still a coward, I discovered, I still dared not say anything - I was still too afraid of Sister Penelope's ever-ready anger and Sister Annette's keenly honed tongue. All I could do was to try to mitigate but that wasn't very successful.

On the fifth day I leapt onto my bike straight after breakfast and sped away as fast as my wheels would turn. The fear, the anger, the desperation, the sorrow had all come back. I pedalled furiously back to Andover, slogging up the hills and swooping down the other side much faster than was safe.

The journey back to Andover took far less time and I was exhausted when I got there. I lay on my bed to let the fatigue ooze out of my muscles. The old, old pain was back and my emotions were far too jumbled to think clearly. After a while I ate the sandwiches and fruit-cake that I should have had for lunch. Then a long, hot bath soothed away the soreness and cramp in my muscles. It did nothing for the pain in my heart. I went to bed.

I had ridden too hard all day to give my emotions any outlet. As I lay on my bed and in my bath they had surfaced. Once in bed they beat at me like a winter gale. The tears which I had held at bay for so long overflowed. Away from all people and safe from disturbance I silently cried myself to sleep.

I renewed my vow to have nothing at all to do with The Haven ever again. As it happened, I never had to because the Children's Home closed the following year, in 1956 - and not before time. Apart from the reasons for our being disorderly in the mid-1940s, The Haven's doors were no longer so tightly shut on what went on inside. Polly's visits to the police; my seemingly useless appeal to the Inspector; weals and bruises seen on children at school; countless other little scraps of information were all adding up, telling the outside world. Perhaps the Inspector at last believed.

Chapter 3

Kith and Kin

"...stood aloof, the scars remaining..."
Coleridge, Christabel, Pt ii

Once my new life began I discovered that my sight wasn't my only difficulty. These were many and various but with one major difference from early years. My fellow-students and people round me weren't creating them. They were putting up with them with kindness if not with understanding. A number of problems sorted themselves out fairly quickly. Others took much longer and making friends was one of them.

Leaving friends behind, forgetting them when they weren't there or had left was a pattern of life for me. Ethel once told me that "when you're with people you're very much with them. When they go away you forget all about them."

Like Kipling's cat I walked by my wild lone but never told nobody. I couldn't make the effort towards real friendship. People often said: "I used to think you were really aloof when I first met you". "It's very difficult to get to know you". They said they could get so far, then they were up against an impenetrable prickly barrier. I needed friendliness, though, and I was "great friends" with the companions of the moment. Once they had gone they had to be replaced quickly.

Companionship worked well. People sent me friendly greetings cards: "This old world is nicer because of you." "Didn't take lessons. Just came natural...liking you." These cards pleased me very much but they puzzled me too. How could anyone like me enough to send me cards like that? They were probably just routine for friends, I thought, and I started sending them myself sometimes.

Miss Ellen had sent me one once. It was at Easter the year after I left school.

> *"An Easter wish*
> *Sincerely spoken;*
> *May all our ties*
> *Remain unbroken."*

That card meant a lot to me and I still have it. My surrogate mother who never was, was already beginning to fade.

Two friends I didn't leave behind. I don't know why. Perhaps they meant a little more to me than most. More than I knew, perhaps? Or was it that, against all deserving, they wanted to keep in touch?

Ethel, my friend from Chorleywood, was one, though she had always kept me at arm's length, which isn't surprising. Besides which, when we left school I also kept my distance against any further risk of betrayal.

The other friend was Mrs Heymann. She had often comforted me at school and was as much a friend as anybody. I went to visit her once or twice in the school's staff house but I didn't go often. There were too many "school" associations and I wanted to leave all that behind. Later, Mrs Heymann retired to a newly-built bungalow in Chorleywood and Lotte, one of her daughters, went to live with her. Now that they were living away from the school I was less reluctant to go to see them. Even so, I was always a bit wary. My clothes and hairstyle - always in the latest fashion - never seemed to please "Mrs Haitch" as I called her. She was always telling me what was wrong with both. Mrs Heymann herself had impeccable taste. She was always well dressed and in perfect style and her naturally curled hair was beautifully cut and coiffured. I, on the other hand, was buying my own clothes for the first time in my life. I was also short of money so I had to buy what I could afford. My first outfit of skirt, blouse and cardigan cost me more than my month's salary. I got £7.15s per month. I was proud of my new clothes - the only ones I had. I had to borrow £1 off Miss Russell to meet basic needs till next pay-day and I couldn't go out anywhere for four whole weeks but I didn't mind. I had my very first set of new clothes chosen by myself. I think Mrs Heymann was trying to teach me what a mother might have taught me but I resented it.

In the Spring after we left PTS for our various hospitals we had the Annual Group Prizegiving. That year it was held at Harrrow School and I was going to collect my prize for Hygiene and First Aid. Who could I ask to come as "family"? There was really only one person I could ask but would she come? With some apprehension I asked Mrs Heymann. I was afraid she would refuse but she said she would be delighted to come. I was proud to have such an elegant guest and Mrs Heymann didn't need to be embarrassed about the clothes I was wearing; I was scrupulously clean and tidy in my uniform.

It was a fine, warm day and it was all very enjoyable. There was someone who was pleased at my success and present to see me accept my reward. Someone who was coming to *me*. That made me very happy. It was better than receiving the prize itself.

I made several "friends" among my nursing colleagues but there were three couples in particular: the Floyds, the Hansens and the Bartons. I went to their weddings and welcomed their babies. I was even godmother to the Floyds' and Bartons' first babies. I intended to be like an aunt to them but I forgot them as soon as I moved away.

I hated weddings; I had no social graces and I didn't know how to behave. I didn't know what to do or how to talk to people. After a couple of glasses of wine I was just uninhibited enough not to care, but I would really much rather not be there. Christenings were different. There I knew what was expected of me. I had been made godmother to one of the children in The Haven and I had been well schooled in the form of the Baptism Service and I knew it by heart. The teas afterwards were a bit difficult to negotiate but it was made easier by being godmother. People came to talk to me; I didn't have to go to them - that was always the hard part. It was starting conversations that I always found so embarrassing and difficult.

I visited the Floyds, Hansens and Bartons quite often and sometimes stayed overnight. On the surface I was relaxed and happy with them but, underneath, was the unending anxiety of doing the wrong thing - and I often did. I never knew what was right or wrong so I usually did whatever was suggested. I waited to be told what to do and if I wasn't told I did nothing. For example, when I was staying with Ethel's parents once, they asked me if I wanted to go to a Quaker Meeting with them on Sunday morning. I went with them, even though I didn't want to; it was better than sitting doing nothing till they came back. The Meeting lasted an hour and apart from singing *Jesus calls us o'er the tumult...* we didn't do anything. We just sat around in silence. Sometimes someone got up and said something but there were no priests and no service. The hour seemed like eternity but at least I didn't have to say things I didn't believe or wonder what to do.

Even though I was friendly with the Floyds, Hansens and Bartons I was still very diffident. I still found it hard to believe that anyone really wanted me as a friend. I lived in a state of suspended animation, walking on eggshells. As these feelings slowly began to fade one small incident immediately resurrected all my insecurity and fear in full force. Since then I have never entirely lost it.

Dora Hansen's husband was a Sales Representative. He always seemed very friendly and helpful towards me and I quite often stayed with them on my days off. Dora had left Harrow Hospital by then. We had had a lovely weekend, walking in the crisp sunshine of winter. We had exchanged Christmas presents "not to be opened till December 25th" and we had really enjoyed ourselves. I was first to go to bed and as I reached the top of the stairs I heard Bernie say: "Why can't she come when I'm not here?" What a sickening shock. All the fear, the feeling of unwantedness, the belief that people only invited me from charity came flooding back. All the happiness of the weekend had gone and I swore that I would never visit them again.

I was too introverted and easily discouraged in those days to think any further than my own hurt. Bernie had recently changed his role and spent much more time away from home so time with his wife was precious and he didn't want it cluttered with a visitor but all I saw was that Bernie didn't like me now that he knew me better. My "hedge of thorns" grew thicker and my mistrust of people, however friendly they seemed, got deeper.

This incident stirred up other feelings which had started to go dormant. They rushed back like white water. I was really nothing more than a hanger-on; a gap-filler. I was always on the outside. Everybody I knew seemed to have someone to share their lives; I had nobody. I couldn't invite people to my home; I didn't have one. Everyone was getting married and having babies. Who needed me? Well, it didn't really matter. I didn't need them, either.

This self-erasure was made slightly better when I shared a flat with the Casualty Sister, Gillian Carr. I was still at Harrow Hospital and a Sister in the Theatre. Gillian was a very pleasant, calm person and we got on well together. She is still a friend. We watched television in the evenings or went to the cinema or something when we were both in. We had our own friends and often invited them to the flat for communal meals. Gill often visited her father on her days off and I usually went away for mine. We even hosted one or two parties. I didn't enjoy them much, I was too shy, but it helped a lot to have Gill there to take the lead. Those were two happy years for me.

Usually I avoided parties on account of my incapacitating shyness but I was to give them up almost completely after a horrifying incident.

I was near-panicked by any kind of social encounter whatsoever. Once I was a staff-nurse my circle seemed to widen and my problems increased with the widening. That was when I found, like many other people, that a drink beforehand often counteracted the shyness and the problems a little. If the social occasion was a big one - like a date - I might even have two drinks. I gradually reached the stage when I never went out without having had at least one. If I had a bottle to hand, that is. I couldn't always afford it. Starting out on a social "do" or a date without a drink first was sheer hell.

One evening the doctors were having a party in their quarters in the hospital grounds. I was on duty in the Theatre. The young house surgeon talked me into going to the party when I came off at 10.30 p.m. and, very reluctantly, I agreed. I went in uniform partly as a joke and partly because I was "on call". I therefore couldn't have a "rave-up" and my uniform would say so.

A young doctor, noted for his practical jokes, put a small shot of neat alcohol into my second drink. It would have been my last before going to bed anyway. It was already near midnight. After that second drink I went out like a light and there was apparently utter consternation all round. I was taken to my room, hardly breathing, by a doctor and two staff-nurses. They even thought of fetching Miss Martin - her house was across the road from our hostel - but they decided against this and a staff nurse stayed with me all night. Someone must have dug my guardian angel in the ribs. "Come on. On your feet. You've done precious little since you were appointed in 1935. Now's your moment to redeem yourself a morsel." My guardian angel must have done his stuff because there was no emergency that night. That doctor gave up practical jokes and I gave up alcohol bolsters; I had been scared out of my wits. That was the first and last time I ever did anything so utterly irresponsible when I was on duty. There had been a second nurse "on call" - there always was - but that was no excuse at all.

Sharing a flat with someone or visiting people only served as a rather ineffectual strapping over a wound which showed no signs of healing. I still desperately yearned to belong somewhere to someone. Thus it was that I made another attempt to join my family; this time my father. I got his address from Miss Russell but my experience with my mother had taught me caution. I didn't rush off to the town where my father lived. In August 1958 I wrote to him. I planned the letter with great care and even more anticipation. I told him that I had always been sure that it wasn't his fault that I was put in the Orphanage.. I knew my mother was wicked and cruel and I didn't ever want to see her. I would like to see him, though, if he would like us to meet. I finished it: Your daughter, Joan

I had no hopes at all. My father might be dead or he might have moved. I posted the letter anyway.

I expected to have to wait a long time for an answer - if I ever got one. To my astonishment it came within a fortnight, on 2nd September, 1958.

"Dear Daughter,"

What a lovely word. A word full of hope and promise.

"I am pleased to hear from you as you have always been in

134

my thoughts since we parted."

It never occurred to me to wonder why, in that case, he had never sent me a single card or letter while I was in the Orphanage.

"...when I put you in the care of those people and I knew you were safe and sound...."

It still didn't enter my head that my father was in any way responsible.

"But now that I have heard from you there will always be a place here and a warm welcome...You must write and keep in touch with me now and some day we shall be seeing each other after nearly 20 years..." I believed every word.

Mentally, I went into Space and dreamed dreams. At last I belonged....Dad....my Dad...A job near him...The door would open....big hugs...I didn't even think about being the spitting image of my mother... as, apparently, I am.

I dreamed through my work all day. The operating theatre was closed for its annual clean and I was working on the Medical Ward. There was no drama or emergency there to bring me back to earth. I smiled and talked to patients; I tended them; I supplied their wants but my heart and mind were up north with my dad...

That evening, when I was free, I wrote the letter which would be the first step to the reunion. It said how wonderful it would be to see him after so long. How we had so much to share. How we would make up for lost time...

I mused as I took my letter to the post. How soon would he write? How soon could I go to see him? His first letter had come in less than two weeks.

My father's answer didn't come in two weeks. It didn't come in two months. It didn't come. I sent him a Christmas card but he didn't send me one. I sent him another letter early in 1959. No answer. I was heart-broken and I felt deserted. Then I remembered. My Dad had said he was expecting to move house. In the hustle and bustle he hadn't been able to send me his new address. Perhaps he hadn't even got my letters and card. Dad had also said in his letter that he hadn't been very well for sometime. Could he be dead? Oh no! Please, no!

I waited nearly a year and kept my dreams alive. Then I wrote to the Registrar for Births and Deaths and the Town Clerk in Dad's home town. The Registrar had no record of my Dad's death and, in her own hand, she wished me the very best of luck. The Town Clerk gave me Dad's new address.

I wrote to the new address. I told him of my other letters and I waited for his answer. And waited... and waited...with dwindling hope. I watched the star over the rubble heap disappear. It had twinkled briefly; then it had been snatched into a Black Hole. I had stood on tiptoe to catch the star and fly away from the rubble. As the sky darkened I sank back into the heap. There was to be no Dad for me.

Chapter 4

At First Sight, Love

"...to some faint meaning make pretence..."
Dryden, Mac Flecknoe, 1,19

The main topic of conversation on and off duty was boyfriends. Everyone seemed to have one and it carried a lot of kudos. Bruce, Mark, Nigel, Bob, parties, dances, "Mum likes him." Broken hearts. Making up. New boyfriend. "Is it serious?" "Oh, what a lovely ring." "When's the happy day?" So many of my friends and colleagues were getting married or engaged to be married after they qualified. I used to talk hard about their love affairs and weddings so that no one noticed that I wasn't talking about my own boyfriend - I thought.

I had about three weeks to go on Men's Surgical - my first ward - when the junior Sister came up to me. "Are you doing anything on Sunday afternoon, Hall?" She must have known that I would be working a 2 p.m-5 p.m. shift. "No," I said, rather mystified. Sisters didn't usually bother about small fry like first-year nurses in their off-duty time. We didn't call each other by our first names either - not on duty anyway. "Would you like to come to lunch with Dave and I? We don't live far away." Sisters and staff-nurses had alternate weekends off - the quietest time of the week. I accepted. I was puzzled, nervous, pleased and flattered. It was the first time anyone had invited me to their home since I'd started nursing.

When Sunday came I didn't want to go. This often happened to me. My nervousness and fear overrode any other feeling by that time and I wanted to cry off. I couldn't avoid it though; this was someone I worked with.

137

When I arrived, there was a fellow guest, a very pleasant young man called Douglas. Nothing went wrong and we had a very good lunch. Much better than hospital food.

About three o'clock Douglas said he'd see me back to the hostel. We chatted freely, at ease in each other's company. It was a fine day so we'd walked quite a bit of the way. At the hostel door I turned to say goodbye. Douglas was suddenly very shy and hesitant and I wondered what was wrong. "Could I see you again?" he asked, as if he expected me to say no. We stood aside for two fellow-students to go in. They looked at us, looked at each other and grinned.

"Well, yes," I answered, "that would be nice." We arranged an evening and Douglas said he would come and pick me up. I said goodbye and went into the sitting room. The two students were there. "Hello, Joan," said one of them. "Was that your boyfriend? You've kept him pretty dark." They grinned at each other and teased me. I was confused and a bit cross. I didn't like people to make fun of me. I went up to my room until it was time for tea.

The word "boyfriend" panicked me. It meant kissing in corners and doorways and I wished now that I hadn't agreed to go out with Douglas again. I had got beyond the stage of thinking it was wrong to talk to boys but I hadn't got any further. I hadn't had the opportunity.

I needn't have worried. Douglas took me to the pictures and was courteous and attentive. I asked him to hold my arm along the dark streets and I was very grateful that he did. It would have been so embarrassing to have one of my usual nightly accidents. During the evening we discovered that we both liked cycling. The following week I had a Saturday off so we planned to spend it together on our bikes. When we got back to the hostel Douglas didn't try to kiss me as I had feared. We just agreed to meet on my next evening off and said goodnight. I was beginning to like having a boyfriend; it wasn't as bad as I had thought it would be.

When we met on the Saturday we cycled over to Thame and stopped at the bridge over the river. Douglas belonged to a cycling club and that day they were having time-trials and Douglas's job was to clock up the time of each cyclist as he came through. Between cyclists Douglas tried to put his arm round me but I moved away from him and I wished I wasn't out with him. After a few unsuccessful attempts he asked: "What's the matter? Surely you don't mind me putting my arm round you?" I didn't say anything. How could I tell him that indeed I did; that it gave me the heebie-jeebies?. Or why.

I sometimes went to the Cycling Club meetings with Douglas when I was free. His friends teased him like mad. "Hey, Doug's got himself a girlfriend at last. When's the happy day, Doug?" Douglas laughed it off but I was embarrassed and a little chagrined. Why couldn't he get a girl before? Didn't girls like him? Was he dating me just because he wanted to be like all his mates? As I did? Was I the only girl who would have him? I didn't understand at all. I began to avoid dates. I pleaded other engagements. Sometimes I just didn't turn up. "Oh, I'm sorry, Douglas. My off-duty was changed at the last minute." I had gone to Women's Surgical by that time, otherwise I wouldn't have been able to play that card.

We still went cycling together. Douglas had bought a tandem some time before I took against him. After that, the boys at the Cycling Club used to sing "Daisy, Daisy" when we arrived and I just couldn't cope with it. I didn't really want to get married and the ribaldry alarmed me.

To my lasting shame Douglas believed my "reasons" for the date-dodging. When we did go out together he was every bit as attentive. I was very friendly to him and kept my real feelings to myself. I had even progressed to letting him put his arm across my shoulders without my shuddering.

> *Put your arms around me honey,*
> *Hold me tight;*

I wanted these songs to mean something to me but the reality was unthinkable. I sang-along with everyone else and they seemed to believe them. Did they really? Why couldn't I? They all had "their" song so I pretended to have mine. I knew about special songs. Someone, I forget who, used to play the piano when I was staying with my aunt and everybody sang. One of the songs was: "Along came Bill ... He's just my Bill." It was apparently my mother's favourite song; Bill was the name of her latest husband. I can't remember the rest of the words. It drove me up the wall and I was glad to get away from it.

The night came when Douglas wanted to kiss me goodnight. It wasn't a passionate clinch; he just put his arms gently round me and his lips touched mine. It never turned into a real kiss. At the first tentative caress I panicked. I pushed him away and fled into the nurses' hostel. Earlier in the day Douglas had said he wanted to marry me. I had smiled at him and said nothing. That soft, silent question on his lips ended what relationship there had been.

Douglas tried for some time to persuade me to go out with him again but I couldn't. I was much too spooked by everything to do with boy-girl relationships. Finally, I took refuge in a lie; another boy-friend. Douglas seemed genuinely upset but I couldn't cope with anyone who wanted more than companionship. I think Douglas must have truly loved me though I can't imagine why. I was as responsive as an armadillo. Douglas was thoughtful and considerate and he left me alone when he knew - or thought he knew - that there was someone else. My only feeling at the time was of having escaped some indefinable threat. The only thing that I actually regretted were the long tandem rides. Cycling on my own was nerve-racking, I couldn't always see traffic signals or read signposts or road directions. That hadn't mattered when there wasn't so much traffic, I had just either stopped or crossed the road to look at them. Neither could I judge the speed of cars and lorries when I wanted to turn right. Tandem-riding took all the worry out of cycling and just left the thrill of it.

There were other boyfriends; Danny, who belonged to the Queens Ice Skating Club in Wembley. He taught me how to skate and gliding round the ice hand-in-hand was exhilarating. He too was a cyclist. Alas; Danny went the way of Douglas as soon as the canoodling started;

> Love me tender, love me true
> All my dreams fulfil;

It was Jimmy who taught me to kiss. It didn't touch me

140

emotionally but everyone was doing it so it couldn't be that bad. I never enjoyed it but I could put up with it. A 'flu epidemic killed that one. I was at the end of my second year of training and about half the ward staff were off sick. When I succumbed the ward was closed to admissions, routine or emergency. My going brought the number down to critical level and when I went back on duty the men all ribbed me. "When Sister and Staff McCleod go off nothing happens. When you go off the hospital comes to a full stop. You must be very important." Men love teasing nurses and it was a huge joke for some time. I loved it.

We had been so short-staffed at the height of the epidemic that the duty roster was often changed without warning. Surgical wards have a lot of emergencies as well as routine admissions and we usually had two or three critically ill patients. When I had had to put Jimmy off three or four times in two weeks he stopped believing in "We're desperately busy. I had to change my off duty." He took it as a put-down, asked me why I couldn't be honest about it and broke it off. I wasn't sorry; he, too, had been getting serious.

When boys started telling me they wanted to marry me I didn't believe them. Even more, I just couldn't contemplate the idea. Caressing, other than kissing, however innocent, was taboo. None of my boyfriends could understand it but how could I admit to my horror. I would see my engaged friends sitting together; the boy would have his arm round his girl, his hand cupped over her breast. They never looked as if they were frightened; they seemed to enjoy it.

Once I almost reached the stage of getting married. I was dating a boy called Nicholas. I was qualified by that time and working in the Operating Theatre. Nicky and I had been going out together for some time and I liked him a lot. We saw each other three or four times a week and we had a lot of fun. We began to talk about marriage. Most of my friends were married or engaged. Babies were appearing at a great rate and I was beginning to feel left out of it all. I didn't feel a great surge of longing when I saw other people's babies but I was already twenty five. I ought really to be getting on with it. Friends were beginning to tell me that. Des Floyd said he'd be my best man. Peer-group pressure was winning.

I had eye tests from time to time, as I had done since I was small. I went for a routine check-up about the time when Nicky and I had agreed to tie the knot. A new eye-specialist had joined the Practice and he did a very thorough examination. When he had finished, he didn't usher me out immediately as usually happened. Instead, he asked me to sit down. "Are you getting married?" he asked. "Yes," I said, wondering why he'd asked. Then, very gently, he asked: "Are you considering having children? "Well, yes." I answered. What a funny question. The specialist was silent for a while. Then, softly, he went on: "Well, I think you should think very hard about that." "Why?" I asked, apprehensively, half-knowing. Memories of Chorleywood flooded back. He looked at me silently and kindly. At last he spoke. "You have a very rare retinal disease. If you have children they may well be born blind. Or they will probably go blind in middle age. It's something you need to think about." Crash! Another K.O. I had come out of my corner ready to fight my fear of marriage and all it meant. What was Nicky going to say?

I didn't tell him at first but I was very edgy. Chorleywood had shown me how well blind people could cope with life. I also knew what hell it could be.

> Scorn us if you will but do not pity us
> For though our world is small and measures but in feet,
> We see the detail of our microscopic world
> And to see the other side we cross the street.
>
> P.J.E.

Yes, but what a nuisance to cross a frighteningly busy street - and find that what you want is on the side you've just left. If my eye disease was very rare perhaps I could make it rarer by not having children. Nursing was about making people better; not giving them disease. I made my decision.

My edginess exasperated Nicky. "Whatever's the matter with you, love? Why are you so scratchy?" I told him. He was very upset. We didn't go to the pictures. We talked instead - for hours; over and over the same ground, looking for a way round it. Adoption? There were lots of children needing new parents. Who knew better than me?   Nicky wanted his own children; not someone else's. There was no way out.

I had thought that I loved Nicky but I don't think I did. I was secretly relieved that there was an outside reason for not getting wed. I don't know if the marriage would have worked. I doubt it because I was still at the stage of "kissing only". I was frightened even of Nicky wanting to touch my breast. I went mad if he tried to open my blouse. "Wait till we're married," I would say, wanting to put off the evil moment. What would have happened when he'd wanted sex on the "happy night" I dread to think. I pretended to everyone that I was heartbroken. I pretended that the song "Magic Moments" was too painful to listen to. It had been Nicky's and my favourite song.

I never let a relationship reach that point again. I didn't really know what love was. I liked a lot of people but I loved no-one. Marriage was not for me.

ACT 2

PHYLLIS

Out of the rubble of life you plucked me
Scratching, biting, unrefined;
You bore no grudge at my hurting ways
But gentled me as you would a hind
That is wounded, needing care.

Into the joys of life you brought me
Slowly, patient, strong in trust
That broken vessels can be restored
Even when their outer crust
Is thick and caked with age.

Now the damage is almost mended;
Dents and cracks are well-nigh gone;
The curing has been a work of love
And little shows, now the task is done,
Of the wounded orphan-child.

Pauletta J Edwards

Chapter 1

Beginnings

"I shall light a candle of understanding within thine heart,
which shall not be put out"

2. Esdras xiv, 25

I was still embedded in the rubble but the sun was shining feebly on my part of it. One or two people had tugged at my hand a little but without much success. Would I ever get out? It was just over a year since the "now-you-see-him-now-you-don't" entrance and exit of my "dad", and when I had finished midwifery I went back to Harrow Hospital. The staff was pretty much the same in the Theatre except that there was a new anaesthetist called Dr Edwards. She was different from any consultant I had ever met. For one thing, she was quite ready to look after herself and didn't expect nurses to wait on her hand and foot. For another, she was the most remarkable person I had ever met.

Dr Edwards - it was to be a long time before I even thought of her as Phyllis - was widely travelled - India, in the RAMC during the war; Denmark after the war with the World Health Organisation, helping the Scandinavians to modernise their anaesthetic practice; Africa, from 1953-59 helping to set up the University of Ibadan. She was full of anecdotes, observations and descriptions and, for me, "abroad" began to have real meaning. In her four years in India and her seven years in Africa Dr Edwards had often given anaesthetics with almost no equipment and had helped to develop a university and its teaching hospital from virgin earth. She had tremendous energy and a very forceful personality and she would give as much attention to a Theatre porter as she would to the chief surgeon. When she saw red tape she cut it and she could always show bureaucracy a quicker way to do something. She was an excellent anaesthetist and I would have trusted her with my life. She could take over a crisis and restore order within a few seconds and she was very supportive of staff members. Two instances stand out particularly in my mind.

Our morning operating sessions usually began at 9.30 a.m. and when she was the anaesthetist, Dr Edwards always came early. One morning, before the routine session began, a small boy came to Theatre with a perforated appendix. I was senior staff nurse and on duty at the time. Fairly soon after the operation had begun the child, who had a high temperature, began to have convulsions. The anaesthetist was one of the local GPs, who were trained to anaesthetise for mostly minor surgery. GPs were quite capable of dealing with an appendicectomy but not with a child having convulsions under anaesthetic.

As the convulsions started, I heard Dr Edwards arrive. I slipped out and quickly explained the situation. I went back into Theatre with Dr Edwards almost on my heels. She had thrown on a gown, cap and mask and she came in "to see what we were doing before the morning session began," by which time she was at the table. "Ice, lots of it." she said. I sent a staff nurse to the kitchen, not very far away, and I notified them that she was on her way. The ice was ready when the nurse got there and within five minutes she was back. Used as she was to running large anaesthetic departments throughout her working life, Dr Edwards taught the GP without taking over from him. They worked together as a team, the convulsions were brought under control and the boy recovered without a trace of his ordeal.

A few weeks later, this incident still fresh in mind, I was called out at about midnight for an emergency - a critically ill patient with an intestinal obstruction. "Who's the anaesthetist?" I asked routinely when I reached Theatre. "Dr Y"., (a G.P.) the Theatre night nurse told me. No G.P., even as good as Dr Y., could have dealt with such a serious operation, I felt. I rang the House Surgeon (nearly two months into his surgical training) and suggested that he call the consultant anaesthetist on call. "Dr Y. is a very competent anaesthetist and, anyway it's none of your business." The House Officer was exceedingly cross. "Please." I said, "Dr Y. isn't trained to cope with this sort of thing." We ought to have a consultant." The consultant anaesthetist was duly called (it wasn't Dr Edwards) and the patient survived. Neither the Registrar nor the House Surgeon spoke to me, except professionally. They were both extremely angry with me.

A few days later I received a letter from the Hospital Administrator to the effect that the choice of anaesthetist was not my affair. My job was to prepare the Theatre and to assist the surgeon. If I interfered in this way again I would be called before a disciplinary committee, which could well cost me my job.

Not many months later I found myself in a similar position. This time Dr Z., again a G.P., was on call and I was not happy. I hesitated. I had always believed that my first loyalty was to the patient... But disciplinary committees... My job...? I finally told the Registrar that I wouldn't "take the case" - i.e. take nursing responsibility for and scrub for it - unless the consultant anaesthetist was called. Luckily for me it was Dr Edwards. Afterwards I told her what had happened and that I was now for the high jump. "Leave it to me." was all Dr Edwards said. There was no disciplinary committee hearing: no sacking; not a word, not even from Dr Edwards. Also, there was never any further problem at night. GPs were no longer called out.

I had had a pretty high opinion of Dr Edwards' attitude and efficiency before that episode. Afterwards I thought the world of her. I knew that the patient mattered to her above all else and that we could rely on her support professionally if we needed and warranted it.

A year after my return to Harrow Hospital I was promoted to Sister. At the end of operating sessions the surgical staff and anaesthetist talked together in the Surgeons' Room. As Theatre Sister I used to be there having coffee with them; real ground coffee, made by the Theatre porter. At first, painfully shy as I was, I said very little, but, very gradually, and encouraged by Dr Edwards, I began to join in the conversation. Dr Edwards was the kind of person who could get anyone to talk. Slowly, she drew me out so that I was even willing to make my own contribution. I had grown to like and respect Dr Edwards for her unfailing good manners as well as her professional ability and efficiency. She taught us all a great deal, from sister to the most junior student nurse, without being heavy-handed. I also learned a lot from her conversations with surgeons. She was a walking encyclopaedia and her tales of her travels were fascinating.

One day, much to my surprise, Dr Edwards invited me to dinner. The idea of a dinner, with guests all high up in their own fields, frightened me out of my wits. I would feel even worse than I usually did whenever I was invited to anyone's home. I was about to refuse when Dr Edwards said: "Do come. There'll only be my mother and I." I was still a bit dubious but thought I could survive with just the two of them. Dr Edwards always made everything sound so easy. I got so anxious over the next few days that I nearly backed out several times but nervous though I was, I went. It wasn't long before I wished I hadn't.

Dr Edwards and her mother were kindness itself. They did their best for me but how could they hope to remould me in one evening? My lack of social graces had never been more apparent and that alone made me as taut as a bow. I knocked over the table decoration and helping myself to vegetables was hazardous. I kept dropping things and I got more and more embarrassed. I was so strung up that I couldn't join in the conversation at all. I needed all my concentration to negotiate the meal. Everything I'd learnt over the last few years had gone.

There was a large Icelandic sheep rug on the hearth and while we were having coffee after dinner I wrapped myself in it. Its' warmth and softness was comforting, rather like a baby with its buddy. In utter disbelief I heard Dr Edwards' mother say: "She looks rather pathetic, doesn't she." I expect I did; I was, after all, twenty-six not six years old. Memories of the Charitable Lady surged back and the remark, perhaps meant to be light-hearted, helped me quite a lot. I didn't spill a single drop of coffee; nor was I rude though I was seething under the surface. I just smiled and said: "Oh, I don't feel pathetic. It's just such a lovely rug." I was busy thinking that I would never go to anyone as high-up as the Edwardses again. I didn't even know what time to go home. When I visited other friends we watched television or played Monopoly or something so I went when we had finished. That was often quite late. If we went to the pictures or a concert the evening came to a natural end. On that evening with the Edwardses there was no natural cut-off and I hadn't had guests of my own at that point. It was getting dark anyway so I didn't know how I was going to get to the station and I was much too shy to say anything. Eventually Dr Edwards solved the problem by offering to drive me there.

Mrs Edwards, I gather, thought I was 'ooden - Devonshire for dull and boring and I should think I was - especially at that first dinner. Professionally I had less of a problem. I was on my own territory and I was the boss. I knew what was what and I was gaining some poise during Surgeons' Room chats. Moreover, if the conversation got difficult I could take myself off to "do some work." I could hardly pluck up the courage to talk to Dr Edwards when I saw her next and I was heartily glad to be wearing a face mask. Until the embarrassment had worn off I avoided her as much as possible, though she behaved as if nothing had happened.

I nearly fell over backwards when she invited me again because I was afraid that I had used up all my approval points. Oh no, I thought, I couldn't possibly go through all that again. I invented excuses for the next two invitations but the third one I accepted. I couldn't go on refusing, and, strangely, I didn't really want to. That second dinner was much less fraught. The table decoration stayed upright; my knife, fork and spoon stayed in my hands and the vegetables went directly from dish to plate. Everything was so much smoother that I took more part in the conversation, greatly helped by my comforter, the Icelandic rug. I left straight after coffee because it seemed like a "natural end" and, all in all, the visit had been a much more successful one. As the visits became more frequent the Icelandic rug became like one of the BOBS. It was my shield and protector until I was easier in Dr Edwards' company.

I never saw Mrs Edwards again. She died soon after that second dinner. Dr Edwards took two or three days off from the operating theatre, then she came back as if nothing had happened. I never knew anyone who could hide her feelings as well as Dr Edwards. I had never seen her moody, miserable, angry or unhappy. When her mother died I realised, that like me, she kept her real feelings deeply submerged. I had written to her officially on behalf of the Theatre staff, the first letter of condolence I had ever written. I knew that it was my function as Sister but, apart from Pudding, death meant nothing to me personally so I had no idea what to say. Nobody had said anything to me when Pudding died, apart from Sister Annette telling me not to be sloppy and that letter to Dr Edwards was one of the most difficult I have ever had to write. When patients died in hospital I had never known what to say to parents or relatives and we were never given any help during our training.

Later on - possibly when Dr Edwards thought I could handle it - I was invited with other guests. By that time I could hold my end up in a conversation with Dr Edwards and the surgeons but with Dr Edwards' friends it was quite a different matter. These people were all leaders in their own fields - nuclear physicists, civil engineers, chief anaesthetists in Denmark and Iceland, doctors, authors, professors. I backslid rapidly. I didn't know when to speak or when to be silent. I didn't know whether what I wanted to say was stupid or intelligent. More disconcertingly, my visual problems came much more into play.

In groups and in a large room, many of the people present are just blurs to a partially sighted person. We don't pick up the look which asks our opinion or invites us to speak. We don't see the encouraging look of interest which shows us we're on the right track or catch the sidelong look between two people which says "Oh, Lord; how boring!" and we sometimes plunge in when the host or hostess has, by a glance, invited someone else to speak. My squint, as in my childhood, often compounded the difficulties in those early days and made me very diffident.

Gradually Dr Edwards' friends began to call me by my name in conversation. I responded and started talking more as I got to know them better and felt more at ease.

Now that she was freer, Dr Edwards began taking me for walks with her. I had missed the walking of my childhood very much but I never went on my own as an adult. I was rather afraid of getting lost. Dr Edwards introduced me to the magic of Kew; the glories of Richmond Park; the pleasures of a long hike over the Downs. These walks were a double delight for I also learned a lot of natural history. For the first time in my life I saw the real joys of Nature. Dr Edwards would show me flowers I had never seen before and would never have caught sight of on my own. I learnt to recognise animal tracks and watch for birds. I had learnt to be observant in my job but in Nature my eyes were no good without Dr Edwards' help. She had a pair of binoculars which she would lend me. Then she would patiently locate something for me; left a bit, up, right, along the branch, down to the left. Suddenly a thrush in full song would spring into view. Magical days.

Eight months after Mrs Edwards died I went to University College Hospital. I went on sharing the flat with Gill, the Casualty Sister, for a few months because travelling wasn't that difficult and I had no problems with getting to work on time. Gill then went to look after her father and I went to live in the UCH staff hostel.

When I left Harrow Hospital I thought I would be leaving Dr Edwards behind. A great pity because I would miss all the magic of the walks and the increasingly pleasing social contact. Deep, deep down, though, I was half-relieved because I was beginning to get too much a part of Dr Edwards' life and she of mine. I liked her very much and enjoyed everything we did - the walks, the concerts, meeting her friends and learning all the time. The break would be a very good thing; I didn't want to get hurt again. Too many people had walked nonchalantly into and as blithely out of my life, wreaking havoc as they went. This time I would be the one to say goodbye.

Chapter 2

Repeat Performance

"Tis a lesson you should heed..."
William Edward Hickson, Try & Try Again.

In the summer of 1963 I began working at University College Hospital in the Theatres. There were three operating rooms and quite often they were all functioning at the same time. In one, though, we only did small operations which didn't take long and which could be cancelled at a moment's notice. We had many emergencies and they often needed immediate treatment to save lives; road accidents, industrial accidents, stab wounds, head injuries, chest injuries, emergencies during pregnancy - my experience widened by leaps and bounds.

To my surprise, after I left Harrow Hospital Dr Edwards did keep in touch since she knew that I hadn't moved house and one evening she invited me to go with her to the Richmond Theatre. There was a play she thought I might enjoy. We agreed that I would stay with her overnight so that I didn't have to travel about in the dark.

I had steeled myself against ever seeing Dr Edwards again and I was delighted at the thought ... at first. Then came a warning, loud and clear. Joan, Joan, think. What are you doing? Remember Miss Roslyn. Remember Miss Ellen ... What makes you think Dr E is any different? A hundred and one things. She actually seems to care what happens to me ... That's just her way. She cares about what happens to anyone, everyone ... She's opening up the world for me. She takes me to theatres, concerts, art galleries ... She can just as easily shut it up again and it will hurt far more. She'll probably go abroad again for years. Then what will you do ...?" I shut out the warnings and looked forward to the visit with pleasure.

It was good to see Dr Edwards again. The dear, familiar house; the view of Kew across the river at sunset; the lovely Icelandic rug which had helped me so much and so often at the start. I had stopped wrapping myself up in it some time ago but now I sat on it. It was still a comfort and support and I loved its smooth, silky texture.

As usual when I went to see Dr Edwards, I put on a record. She never minded; on the contrary, she always encouraged me. One of my favourite records was Beethoven's Septet in E and I played it often. It is a very calming piece of music and calm was what I needed more and more as the years went by.

I stifled my fears and continued to enjoy life. I could take it or leave it and when the time came ... Well, Ethel and the Heymanns hadn't dented my armour, had they? I was the cat that walked by itself and all places - and people - were alike to me.

In the Autumn of 1963 Drs Merab and Leon Tauman, friends of Dr Edwards and both professors at the University of West Australia, came to Europe. Between visits here and there they spent short periods with Dr Edwards. I met them a few times while they were with her and I enjoyed their company immensely.

One evening Leon said he wanted to go for a walk. Would Paulette like to go with him? "Leon," said Dr Edwards, "I said her name was Joan Hall, not Paulette." "Ah," answered Leon, "but Paulette suits her so much better." We all laughed and Dr Edwards, influenced by the Italian, called me Pauletta for fun. She has an Italian cousin by marriage and an Italian friend who was her anaesthetic orderly in India and she loves Italy. Thereafter the Taumans and Dr Edwards called me "Paula" as a joke but gradually it ceased to be a joke for me. I began to call myself Paula until I was Paula to everyone except officially. I had a new identity. When Dr Edwards called me "Pauletta" it gave me a sense of belonging. It gave me mother-feelings about her, which frightened me. Miss Roslyn ... Miss Ellen ... beware Paula. I was beginning to let myself care about Dr Edwards. I went on enjoying the walks, the concerts, the weekends, the social occasions with her numerous friends but behind it all was a new sense of unease and fear. I tried to ignore it.

Then a chill set in. Friends began to say: "Phyllis, when are you going abroad again? You haven't been home this long (five years) since I've known you." Denmark, India, Africa, where next? "Oh, any day now," Dr Edwards would answer breezily. "Now that Mother's not here there's nothing to stop me." The first time I heard such an exchange it was like being hit with a sandbag. I knew it! Dr Edwards, like all the rest, was going to leave me flat. She had trotted into my life and now she was going to trot out again. I had let her get closer to me than anyone before and it was all going to go up in smoke. "You've got to stop it - and quick", I told myself. Get out before you're pushed out. All right. She's given you what you've never had before ... a sort of home. She's almost like a ... Oh, don't be ridiculous. Who needs a *mother* at 28. Paula ... Pauletta ... You like that ... Yes, well, she always sounds as if she cares when she's looking after someone who she thinks needs help. What good will it be when she's no longer there? Perhaps she'll write ... Oh, yes! I should be so lucky. That never worked before. Once she goes abroad she won't give me a second thought.

Day after day I waited for the casual "Oh, Pauletta, I'm off to Timbuktu for ten years next week..." I couldn't bear it. I had to end it all now; not just wait for it to happen.

In December Dr Edwards invited me to spend Christmas with her and the Taumans. At first I was delighted and accepted with real pleasure. I asked for the time off and looked forward to Christmas with anticipation. Then my dislike of other people's Christmases, the sharing, the hugging and kissing, took over. I'd be left out. The thought of it all heightened my disquiet and my resolve.

On December 22nd I went to Dr Edwards for the evening. Much more casually than I felt, I said: "I'm sorry but I can't spend Christmas with you. I'd forgotten I promised to spend it with some friends." "Oh dear, what a pity, The Taumans will be disappointed." Dr Edwards answered, "We were so looking forward to your coming." She really did sound disappointed.

I spent Christmas with some friends who wouldn't have family visiting them. The last thing I needed was somebody else's family. I didn't really want to spend it with anybody but Dr Edwards might find out if I didn't. I felt ashamed enough as it was and very unhappy.

Dr Edwards would never have done anything like that and I knew she'd never want to see me again. That was what I wanted anyway ... wasn't it? Dr Edwards knew something about my background by that time and I was sure that the Christmas invitation, like all the others, was just a kindly gesture. At that time I looked on her rather as a patron. "Pauletta hasn't got anywhere to go for Christmas. Let's invite her here." Now here I was throwing it back at her. Well, that would be the end of everything ... I really had put the kibosh on it all ... and none too soon. It wasn't a very nice way to have done it though.

That Christmas was the worst I had ever spent. For one thing, I had a severe cold and the most dreadful tummy upset. I couldn't enjoy Christmas; I was too ill and too unhappy. Even so, I was glad, of course, that I had plugged the gap in my defences in time. Dr Edwards had been chipping away at them but I knew I had to rebuild them. During Christmas, though, the misery and the regret completely drowned out the relief. I went back to work tired, wan and wretched. I smiled cheerfully and told everyone what a wonderful time I had had. "You must have done," they said drily, "You look like it was some party!".

As well as the urgent need to close up my defences, there was another reason for wanting Dr Edwards out of my life. Earlier in the year I had learnt that Dr Edwards was a Quaker. I had the weekend off and was staying with her. On Sunday we were going for a picnic but Dr Edwards was going to a Quaker Meeting first. It would be silly to make her go all the way home again just to fetch me so I said I would go with her.

When Dr Edwards had first mentioned Meeting my heart sank. She hadn't seemed like a God-person at all and I wasn't going to get inveigled into this Quaker business. I hadn't understood a thing in Bournville except that they were God-people and I didn't want any more of *them* in my life. When we arrived at the Meeting House I found that I already knew quite a few of the people there. I had met them at Dr Edwards' house and I liked them; they were charming people. Come to that, so were Rose and Wilfred Beswick, Ethel's parents.

Everyone sat down and stopped talking. Gradually a deep silence fell and I got immersed in it myself. I was much more aware of the nature of the silence than I had been at Bournville but I resisted it at first. However, I soon found that there was nothing to push against and I felt drawn into it. Dr Edwards was wearing a CND badge (Campaign for Nuclear Disarmament) and I began thinking about war and peace and the nuclear bomb. At some point someone got up and said almost exactly what I was thinking. It was uncanny. No; I wasn't having anything more to do with any religious sects - ever.

Now, by cutting Dr Edwards out of Christmas and out of my life I was scotching trouble all round. My feelings were in total disarray.

To my utter astonishment Dr Edwards invited me for the weekend just after New Year. Leon was going back to Australia the following week so perhaps I would like to come for his farewell dinner? Oh dear. Dr Edwards didn't seem to bear me any ill-will over the Christmas fiasco. She sounded her usual friendly, welcoming self. What was I to do? How could I ditch someone who didn't know that she was being ditched? I had never met anyone like Dr Edwards, who never saw any bad in anyone - at any rate, not in the people she looked on as friends. She had to be pretty convinced before she saw it in anyone else either and even then she would make excuses for most people.

I thought I might as well go since these visits and outings wouldn't continue much longer if Dr Edwards really were going abroad. I could still enjoy the fun and companionship without getting involved.

The first time I went after that awful Christmas I went with a mixture of embarrassment, guilt and apprehension. Pleasantness on the phone was one thing but how would Dr Edwards be when we actually met? In the event, she behaved as she always did - with courtesy, friendliness and welcome. There was no overt indication of having been put out; no hidden resentment either, as far as I could see. The Taumans, too, welcomed me in their own courteous and heart-warming fashion. There was no mention of Christmas. I couldn't understand it. I think that Dr Edwards, in her generosity, must have put it all down to bad management on my part and she didn't hold it against me. For something where I justly deserved to lose all approval points I didn't seem to have lost any.

We had a lovely weekend together. I was Paula ... Paulette ... Pauletta again and I felt as if Dr Edwards and the Taumans really were happy that I was with them. I shut out any feelings about Dr Edwards going away and lived for the moment.

By this time Dr Edwards knew that I couldn't see in the dark or dim light. When we went to a concert on the Friday or walked along the towing path after dark she took my arm to prevent me from coming to harm. That gave me the feeling of being protected - like the Icelandic rug did. It made me feel like I had in the Orphanage when I wanted someone to cuddle me; like I had when I saw mothers being protective towards their little ones.

When I went back to work I felt strangely at peace with the world. There had been no talk of Dr Edwards going away and I was thankful. Yet I was afraid. She already meant far more to me than anyone ever had before and I was learning that feelings can't be held in abeyance to order.

Over the next few weeks I saw Dr Edwards quite often and I resurrected the idea of further study to polish up my brain. The more I saw of Dr Edwards' friends the more inadequate I felt - though they never even hinted that I was. Dr Edwards and I were thinking along the lines of a Bachelor's Degree.

One day in March I was "scrubbed" for a long list. We were on the last operation, it was nearly 3.30 p.m., I was off duty then and going to Dr Edwards for the weekend. The Taumans and a Danish friend of Dr Edwards would be fellow guests. With a little help I could cope with meeting new people by then, so it would be interesting to meet Inge, a fellow nurse.

Towards the end of the operation the Theatre Sister came in. There was a life-threatening emergency - a woman with an ectopic pregnancy. Could I possibly stay? There was no-one else on duty senior enough to take the case. How sickening! Yes, all right, but would she please ring Dr Edwards for me?

We had started on the emergency when Sister could eventually make the phone call. She came back into the Theatre and pulled the rug from under my feet. "Someone called Tauman answered. There's been an accident. Dr Edwards is in hospital. They think she's fractured her spine." Oh, no, no, NO. My heart sank like a lift with a broken cable. "What happened?" I whispered back, still with my eye on the operation. "Sister, could you spare us a minute?" snapped the surgeon. He was right. With my heart thumping like a sledge-hammer I concentrated on the operation. At the end, I handed the patient over to the ward nurse, changed out of my theatre garb in record time and hurtled to Euston Square Underground.

I sat in utter desolation in the train. I felt far worse than when my mother had refused to see me or when Pudding had died. This time there was actually someone to lose. Miserably I thought back to Christmas and how gradually Dr Edwards - or Phyllis, as I thought of her to myself - was getting behind my hedge of thorns. She never seemed to take any notice of obstructions in her way. She either moved them or just walked round them.

How badly was Phyllis hurt? Would she be crippled for life? I struggled to keep calm. It was as if it had happened to my own mother. I let in the thought in all its fullness at last. Phyllis was, would always be my mother. I was Pauletta, Phyllis's daughter. She didn't, she wouldn't ever know. I didn't even have the right to think it. Waves of anger, grief and pain broke over me. Anger that the mother I had finally found had been snatched away. I had at last admitted her to my mind as well as to my heart and now she was gone. I was being tossed about in a maelstrom of emotions I had never felt before. Only with Pudding had I felt anything like love. Even with Phyllis I had hardly dared to admit to myself that I loved her as a mother. I had dammed it all up. Now the floodgates had opened and my pent-up feelings burst out in an uncontrolled torrent. I knew now that I had to be part of Phyllis's life and she mine and look what had happened. The first time that I had ever trusted anyone enough to let them anywhere near my still, silent pool and whoosh! She had dived into the water.

After a sleepless, fretful night, I went as soon as possible to the hospital to see how Phyllis was. She was lying on her back, desperately pale and wan, but smiling and cheerful as usual. "Ah, Pauletta. How kind of you to trudge all the way over here. You mustn't wear yourself out on my account." A frantic thought flashed through my mind. Did that mean that she didn't want me to come?

Oh don't be stupid I told myself as I smiled at Phyllis. "Hello, Dr Edwards. It's no trouble at all. How are you? Do you need anything?" "Why don't you call me Phyllis." she answered, "Haven't we known each other long enough? She picked up a pile of letters from beside her. "This is a marvellous opportunity to catch up on letters." She handed me six. "Could you post these for me?" Phyllis wrote 120 letters during the six weeks she was in hospital.

On my way to work my thoughts were at sixes and sevens. My spirits had soared when Phyllis had invited me to use her first name but they sank equally fast once I had time for reflection. At first I was afraid that I wouldn't be able to cope if Phyllis were permanently disabled. I was sure that I would run away from it all. Having, at long last, unharnessed my tightly reined-in feelings, I was totally dependent on Phyllis. I don't think that then I had the emotional strength to give her what she would have needed. My hold on our relationship was much too fragile for it to stand the strain of dependence on me. How ironical that both these things should happen at the same time.

I was always cheerful when I went to see Phyllis and, I felt, I could at least look after her while she was in hospital. I went every day and I enjoyed being able to take her what she needed or wanted. After a few days she told me that her spine wasn't broken; she had a slipped disc. I was so glad that I hadn't turned tail and fled.

Phyllis duly came home from hospital but it took her weeks to recover and I went to see her often. She had so many friends that she wouldn't have been uncared for in hospital but I had looked after her too. It had been wholehearted, as it had been with Pudding, and somehow something had changed. I felt a little closer to Phyllis and a tiny bit more confident. Not much but enough for me to take a step that was to shake my life to its very foundations. I wrote a letter.

Phyllis was away convalescing and we wrote to each other as usual. I seem to have a built-in urge to self-destruct and one day it came into play in full force. I had written several letters and just had time for one to Phyllis before I went to work. I missed her a lot but I didn't tell her so. I chatted on in the usual way, then: "Take care of yourself. You're the nearest I'll ever come to having a Mum."

It was late by this time so I shoved the letter into an envelope and set off for the hospital. As I passed a pillar box I dropped all the letters in without even stopping. I just caught a train as the doors were shutting and sank into the nearest seat.

Something slammed into my solar plexus. What a buffoon! What had I done? Had I learnt *nothing* over the years? Sister Penelope's words came back in all their horror. Oh God. Perhaps the letter would get stuck in the box, lost in the post, delivered to the wrong address, best of all "Return To Sender". This time I'd put the boot in myself. Why couldn't I just leave things alone; enjoy what I had? Not only had I put my thoughts into words, I had sent them to Phyllis. I knew *I* thought of her as my mother but she didn't - or hadn't. She might not even want to be a pseudo-mother. She could, of course, just ignore it - it was offhand enough - but Phyllis wasn't like that. Thank heaven I was soon going to France. If Phyllis really did think I was off my head I could just get lost. If she didn't want any more to do with such an idiot I needn't write to her in France. I could just forget about her ... bye-bye. This was unthinkable.

A few days later Phyllis's handwriting lay on the doormat. I picked up the letter but didn't open it. I was too busy just then. I made myself some coffee and tried to do the Guardian crossword. It was uncommonly difficult that day... I stopped fooling myself. Let's read the wretched letter and know the worst. After all, what could Phyllis do that others hadn't done before her? What indeed.

I opened the letter, prepared for the biggest put-down of all time. "Don't worry. You've been there before." I told myself bracingly. Had I? I read the letter ... then re-read it. It didn't ignore. It didn't chide. It didn't condemn. It didn't humiliate. Phyllis described the growth of relationships in her own inimitable style: "... something that is born as if by chance, grows unheeded and flowers gently ..." She finished with the ... for me immortal ... words: "Perhaps I need a daughter as much as you need a Mum."

Chapter 3

So Near and Yet So Very Far

Faithful are the wounds of a friend.

Proverbs, xxvii, 6.

At last. After almost three decades of searching and longing I had a mother of my own. Someone to care for me and about me. Someone to say: "How did you get on?" and really want to know the answer. Life could hold no greater gift.

The exchange of letters didn't actually alter anything - except inside me. I gradually began talking about "my mother" to new people in my life but not with anyone else and Phyllis still introduced me as her friend. When I went to work in France in August I could talk freely about "ma mere", "maman". It was like a dream and I didn't want to wake up in case it all went away.

I had arranged to go to France for a year in order to improve my French but when the time came for me to leave I was taken with a sudden reluctance. I had always been ready to pack my bags and leave without a backward glance. Now I needed to stay with Phyllis; I wanted her to hold my hand; I wanted her to hug me but I didn't dare to even hint at these new feelings, which were accentuated by my imminent departure. I doubt if I could have put it all into words at the time, anyway. I knew it wasn't "normal" at my age - I was twenty-nine years old. Like a child I needed reassurance all the time because Phyllis often helped people over difficulties then they faded away. I didn't want to dissolve away like them and I only half-believed in having a mother. People don't usually adopt each other when they are adults. I had never been a child; now I didn't feel like a grown-up.

The still, silent pool had not been quiet for a long time. Phyllis was planting flowers on its banks and I couldn't stop her. I didn't even want to but I was mortally afraid that she would cease to tend them. What would happen if she went away and the flowers died of drought and neglect? That place was taboo to everyone else and I didn't wholly trust Phyllis there.

While I was in France Phyllis was every bit the mother I wanted her to be. She wrote often and she sent words and gifts of comfort when I had my tonsils taken out in January. I was disappointed that I wasn't in England at the time so that Phyllis could visit me in hospital though the nuns and doctors in the Clinique were kindness itself and I couldn't have asked for better care. The nuns knew Phyllis's handwriting by then and one of them would bring a letter: "Voici, "Mees", une lettre ... de votre maman". They called me "Mees" (as in "peace") as a kind of nickname. They had tried to say Miss Hall but very quickly shortened it to "Mees".

The Clinique where I worked was in Normandy. It was staffed by nuns from the nearby Convent of the Sacred Heart and they were marvellous people to work with. They were not all trained nurses but they cared for their patients with loving kindness and compassion. I taught them basic nursing skills and, sometimes, when the doctors came across something unfamiliar they would ask: "Qu'est-ce que c'est?" (What's that?) "Ah," the nun in charge would say: "ça, c'est une affaire de Mees." Even though I missed Phyllis terribly it was impossible not to respond to the warmth and friendliness of the Clinique staff, from the owner to the femmes de chambre. There was a lot of laughter and my homesickness was unseen.

Every week I had a half-day and day off as in England. I always took my half days off but worked my days off so that I could save them for short trips to England. In this way, I took six days at Christmas to spend with Phyllis - and what a Christmas that was. Quite different from the previous year. Everyone was getting used to my being part of Phyllis's life now so whenever Phyllis was invited, so was I. I went back to France warmly enfolded in a very new and exciting sense of being part of a family.

Five days after I had my tonsils out I had an entrance examination for a London college. Not surprisingly, I failed it. Four more university colleges turned me down flat; two others didn't answer my application and I faced the fact that I wasn't going to get in anywhere. Then Birkbeck College, University of London, invited me to sit their entrance exam in September. I passed it.

I had been writing to Ethel all the year. We were in much better contact now and we agreed to share a flat in Highbury, which we did for two years.

My growing love for and trust in Phyllis was beginning to change my attitude and behaviour towards other people. I was learning to relate to others on my terms as well as on theirs and I was more ready to keep in touch. Phyllis was slowly building up my confidence and beginning to sew together my shredded self-esteem.

There was one side of me, however, which got worse rather than better. I forgot or ignored arrangements with other people whenever I felt threatened or apprehensive and needed reassurance.

By early 1967 it was likely that Phyllis was going abroad again to India on a lecture tour for the World Health Organisation. By the end of March it was certain. Also, sometime in the same year the University of London had approached her. They wanted her to go overseas for them again and this time she had a choice. She chose Ahmadu Bello University in Northern Nigeria because a friend of hers was already working there.

This was during the second year of the Degree course and it was all highly unsettling for me. It was hard for me to concentrate on my studies and I almost gave up. My fear that Phyllis would "go to Timbuktu for ten years" had eased off as time passed with no sign of it actually happening. Now, out of the blue, it was back in full force.

I was sure that Phyllis would write at the start; she had shown her capacity for letter-writing during my year in France and whenever one of us was away. Would she want to continue - and would she have the time - when she was head of a Department of Anaesthesia which she was going to Africa to create? I doubted it. My slender trust in the permanency of relationships was already shrinking and the night when I heard about India I had the first of what were to become frequent nightmares of disintegration. I was walking up a spiral staircase. Without warning, the last few steps shattered and fell away. Panic-stricken, I turned to run down again. All the steps behind me were breaking up and disappearing. I was marooned, high up and in almost total darkness. There was no way out. I woke up terrified.

At that point the little girl in me took centre stage but always behind tightly closed curtains and there she stayed for a very long time.

I saw Phyllis as often as possible before she went away. I talked, apparently cheerfully, about the two assignments - and I spent the week-end with her before she went to India.

The following week I received the second of two letters from Mrs Heymann. There was pain and hurt in it:

My Dear Johannchen,
(still the endearment)
Another weekend came and went without you and without any "sorry". Why don't you let us know when you aren't coming?... If you want our friendship to last you will have to mend your ways... we can't keep a whole weekend for someone who doesn't come, not even Johannchen.

Yours sorrowfully,
Gertrud Heymann.
(instead of: "Lots of love, Mrs Haitch").

I was genuinely contrite for treating the Heymanns so shabbily. I never did that again and they now count among my dearest friends. Others gave me what I deserved. They cut me off and I never heard from them again.

During 1965-6 Phyllis had also begun crystallising a long-cherished idea to build a guest-flat over her garage at the end of her garden, which was thirty foot long. Early in 1967 the plan was finalised and discussions started with the architect. When Phyllis told me about it I thought what fun it would be to live there when I was staying with her. "No," said Phyllis; "it's not going to be for guests. It's for you, your home." I was astounded, overcome, by the incredible gift of a home of my own, living so near to Phyllis, being part of her life.

Work started on the building in the summer of 1967 but, with the usual sort of delays, it wasn't finished until early in 1968. In the September of 1967 Phyllis, a great one for making celebrations, arranged the "laying of a foundation stone." We bought a piece of green Welsh slate and had it suitably inscribed in gold lettering by a local mason. "You're the Latin scholar," said Phyllis, (my subsidiary subject at university was Latin) "you plan the wording." With great delight I wrote:

HUNC LAPIDEM POSUIT
EUNICE LOCKEY
(Eunice Lockey laid this stone)
19th SEPT 1967

Dr Eunice Lockey was the Chief Pathologist at the National Heart Hospital and a great friend of Phyllis's.

We invited a few more friends, among them the Stuarts and their children, Adam and Sarnia. Little Sarnia, aged six, presented Eunice with a posy of flowers with deftness and style and I was proud that they had all come to share this moment of great gladness with me.

It was exciting to watch the building rising slowly out of the ground and when Phyllis ceremoniously handed me the key I clutched it tightly in my hand so that I didn't drop it.

Being my third year at university I was a full-time student - which Birkbeck's charter permitted. Otherwise its students had to be in full-time employment. All through the day I studied feverishly, trying to catch up on what I had been unable to do during the first two years. We still had lectures from 6 pm - 9 pm, Mondays to Thursdays so I hardly saw Phyllis in the evening during the week. Also, she was still working at Harrow Hospital so she wasn't home very often in the daytime. At weekends, though, I thought we would be living as a family. I was coming a little further out from behind my hedge all the time but, like a hedgehog, I was ready to roll up tight at the least provocation.

I rolled up tight again soon after I moved into my new home. Phyllis and I hadn't discussed how we would live and to what extent we would share our lives. I suppose that we both thought we knew and it didn't occur to Phyllis that I didn't. She says she would have helped me if she had known. She would come up the garden to tell me that she was going for a walk and I took that to be an invitation to go with her; or to Kew Gardens and I would offer to go too. On such occasions Phyllis would always say something like: "Oh, that would be nice." I didn't know then that that was just a "social noise"; I didn't know that I shouldn't have offered. In any case, I was so dependent on Phyllis emotionally in those days that that I wasn't very sensitive to her needs, quite apart from the fact that I needed to be with her even when it wasn't always possible. My anxiety that she might vanish like the mother of my nightmare had become a dominant factor in my life.

One day Phyllis came to tell me that she was going to work in the garden. When I went to help her, she said: "When people live in a family they don't necessarily spend all their time together. When my mother was alive she and I often went our own ways and I think you must learn to do likewise." I was stunned. I was also mortified and angry. Why did Phyllis bother to come and tell me she was going to Kew or for a walk if she wanted to go by herself? I didn't ask her these questions. I wrapped them up in my yearning and my pain and hid them away.

It was Ethel who answered that question for me. I was staying with her in her flat in London and one day she said: "It's very odd living with you." "Why?" I asked, puzzled. "Well, you never leave notes." was her explanation. "What about?" I asked, totally mystified. "Well, you know. To say you've gone shopping. Or so-and-so rang while I was out. That sort of thing. I suppose you've never really had to do it, have you." but that was eight years later.

In order to make her point, Phyllis kept herself to herself for a while and I, like the hedgehog, went into hibernation. In my new role as daughter this all left me floundering. I had lost my new identity overnight and I didn't really know what my function was.

This new development meant for me: "Keep out of my life unless you're specifically invited." Living yet not living with Phyllis I never knew when or whether I should be with her and her apparent rejection of me cut me like a knife. Why had she given me a flat near her if she didn't want me? Why did she tell me what she was going to do if we were supposed to live separate lives? I thought I understood how families lived but I had obviously got it all wrong. The strange longing, which was to dog me for years, for the regimented life of the Children's Home, where every minute, every action, was governed by decree, came swirling back.

When Phyllis had friends visiting she would usually invite me as well. Until I met her I wasn't used to helping but I had begun to when I thought I was family. Now, with specified rules but which I didn't understand, I didn't know what to do. I saw myself as a guest again, not as a daughter - the daughter business was a figment of my imagination - and I began to behave like a visitor. I didn't do anything unless I was asked in case I was doing the wrong thing. I never asked Phyllis for guidance. I was much too diffident.

This "rejection" happened fairly soon after I moved into my new flat and it almost immediately led to problems. I needed a very small fridge and we hadn't yet found one. The whole flat was 16' x 9' and the kitchen was diminutive. I hadn't yet developed the habit of consulting before taking decisions - but I was learning. Now, with the new rule, I thought I shouldn't bother Phyllis so I bought a small fridge by myself. Fairly soon afterwards, when Phyllis had invited me for a meal, I told her about the fridge and asked her if she would like to see it. She was clearly hurt that I hadn't included her in the choosing. "No," she said shortly, "It's yours. You chose it. I don't need to see it". It was exasperating as well as hurtful. If I did something it was wrong; if I didn't do it it was wrong and I never knew which course of action to take.

This uncertainty and longing caused me a totally unexpected problem. Jealousy. I was jealous of those who needed Phyllis's help, though one family in particular gave me most trouble. These were the Mukherjees. Phyllis had met the wife, Margaret, in India and had invited her to visit when she came to England. She did; so did her husband, Trilokesh. I feared Trilokesh most because he needed a lot of emotional help. Margaret I was most jealous of because she fitted in so easily. She had no difficulty in talking to Phyllis and she slipped so comfortably into the niche that I was trying, with so little success, to fill. I once baby-sat for Margaret while she went for a walk with Phyllis. I could have gone on the walk too but I was certain that Phyllis and Margaret would talk about India and Trilokesh and I would be left out so I stayed with the baby Jayanta - thereby cutting off my nose to spite my face. It was my birthday and when Phyllis and Margaret came back from their walk we had a very pleasant dinner party. There wasn't the faintest suspicion that I was fuming at Margaret for having ruined my birthday, as I saw it. As usual, I kept my feelings to myself - which was always more than half the trouble - and the vortex, on the edge of which I was to hover for twelve long years, began to spin. I was thirty-two years old.

Chapter 4

Climbing The Ladder

" ... yet fear I to fall."

In the summer of 1968 I took a Lower Second B.A. Honours Degree in French. Phyllis was delighted and immediately rang all our friends. She also arranged a celebration and Robert and Lettice Stuart, who lived nearby, came with us to the theatre. In spite of our difficulties, I still had my "someone special" to care about what I did and how it went.

Now what to do? I didn't want to go back to the Operating Theatre and the intellectual restrictions of nursing. A teaching qualification would open many doors and would give me time to plan, I thought. The Department of Modern Languages at the Institute of Education, of the University of London, said they would take me on their Postgraduate Certificate in Education course in 1969 provided that I went to France for a year. Nursing, they said, was too limiting language-wise. I still have a book which was given to me by one of our patients in France, Mme Touroule-Chevallerie. Her husband was a well-known expert on Norman antique furniture and Mme T.-C. and I had long discussions about it. Ah well.

I eventually got a job as an Assistante (English teacher) in Paris for January, 1969 and there began a dreadful six months. The Lycée classes were all unruly after the May riots of 1968; I hadn't found accommodation I could afford so I eventually lived in a cheap hotel; I had a stomach upset for much of the time so was drained of strength and I wasn't allowed to cook, or even eat, in my hotel room so I very seldom had proper food. Against the rules, I had a tiny "Camping Gas" so I could make myself a hot drink and I occasionally boiled an egg but I didn't want to waste the gas. The canisters were very expensive.

All this led to an adult version of my childhood nightmare when my mother disappeared. I dreamt that Phyllis had died. It was a far worse nightmare than the earlier one and I was crying when I woke - and I went on crying. I just couldn't shake off the intolerable sense of loss. I wrote to Phyllis, leaving out the nightmare, and our relationship took a giant stride forward as a result. Phyllis rang immediately to find out what was really the matter and I was at such a low ebb that it all came tumbling out. Phyllis offered both sympathy and practical advice. Then she said: "Would you like me to come to Paris?" I was bewildered. "What do you mean?" I asked. "I could come tonight if you want me to." Phyllis was saying. I still couldn't take it in. "Do you mean to say that you would pack your bags and catch the next plane to Paris? Just like that?" "Of course." Phyllis answered, as if it went without saying. Such an idea was totally alien to me. Could Phyllis really care for me so much that she would come to my aid at the drop of a hat wherever I was? "Any time, day or night, just ring. I'll come over." Phyllis added. My mental backbone straightened. Phyllis meant it and I believed her. I was ready to face the world again. Phyllis made me promise that I would ring her if things got out of hand again. I promised and she told me to reverse the charges.

With one last tug Phyllis had pulled me out of the rubble. She had collected up the pieces with great care but it would take a lot of patience to put them together. It was also going to take a very long time. For the moment, though, I was wrapped in a cocoon of love and care and I knew I would hold out till the end of my time in Paris.

Phyllis sent me some more money and with it I bought a radio. I needed it, even though I hardly had enough to live on. I could now listen to music.

In February Phyllis came to see me on her way to Nigeria. She was going, initially she said, for two years. Her coming coincided with my having Asian 'flu and I was very ill. Phyllis decided that I needed proper care and attention and managed to get a seat for me on the 10.45 p.m. plane out to England that night. It was the only plane on that day because Linden Johnson had been inspecting Concorde and the airport had been closed. How Phyllis got me on to that plane was a miracle but then Phyllis can always work miracles when she has to. She told the airport officials that I had to go on compassionate grounds, she persuaded them to take an English cheque - not at all easy in 1968 - and she got a doctor to sign a certificate to the effect that I needed two weeks' convalescence "in the country." She also arranged for me to stay with the Stuarts when I arrived in England. Later she came to the airport with me and, against all her inclination, she stayed with me until I went through to the Departure Lounge. Phyllis will take anyone anywhere but she seldom waits for take-off, be it plane, train or bus. This time she stayed with me to make sure that I was fit to travel but more to comfort me. She told me not so long ago that she knew that I was very unhappy about her going to Africa, though she didn't know all the reasons why.

I looked on that fortnight off sick as a blessed relief from being an assistante. As I hadn't informed the right person in the Sécurité Sociale in writing about leaving my Paris address my pay for those two weeks was docked. Assistantes only just earned enough to live on, anyway, so I lived in penury till the end of June. In all this my fellow-Assistante Ruth and her friend Janet were Good Samaritans indeed. They looked after Phyllis while she was in Paris and, when I went back, they gave me a good meal from time to time. Even greater gift, they gave me their friendship, sadly lacking to strangers in large conurbations.

In spite of the hardships life got better. My classes settled down and were a pleasure to teach. Mme Hébert, patronne of the hotel, let me hold over payment when I was 'short'; I had told her of the problems with the Social Security. When I left at the end of June I tried to thank her. "Ah, beh! Ces Parisiens, eh?" Mme Hébert dismissed the whole of Paris and all its inhabitants with a flick of the wrist. She was from the Midi. She had often given me a second breakfast and this had given me strength when I had had to walk the seven kilometres to the Lycée. She had kept my room for me, without payment, while I was away with Asian 'flu and she had helped me in so many ways to get back on the level. I will always owe her an enormous debt of gratitude.

At the end of that wasted six months in Paris I went to Nigeria for eight weeks, where Phyllis was settled at Ahmadu Bello University as Dean of the Faculty of Medicine. I shared her flat with her but saw very little of her at first for, as well as being Dean, she was in charge of the Department of Anaesthetics. This she was building up at the same time as teaching and giving anaesthetics, often being called out for emergencies at night.

Then I was asked to teach English and General Studies at the School of Nursing. General Studies was carte blanche and the students and I explored any and every topic they wanted to raise.

Later, I went with Phyllis on some of her visits to Government hospitals and I saw and learnt a lot. The eight weeks in Nigeria taught me how much building there was to do in developing countries. I had read it all in Phyllis's vivid letters but seeing it for myself really brought it home to me.

My increasing trust in Phyllis and the new sense of security I felt was gradually feeding into my other relationships. My protective coating was becoming latticed and I was much more open to friendship and love. Phyllis was on easy terms with all her male friends and I was learning to be with men without feeling threatened. It was Caesar who helped me most in this respect.

Caesar was a Health Services Planner, an idealist who felt that he could help developing countries in many ways. He had been in Nigeria for three years and already had several projects in hand. Like Oxfam, he believed in teaching people how to fish rather than giving them fish to eat.

Caesar visited Phyllis fairly often, both professionally and socially and their discussions were lively and to the point. I listened intently, for it was a new and exciting world they talked of and I absorbed far more than I realised at the time. Caesar was about fifty years old and had worked in several countries before Nigeria so he could compare various health services and take the best from each.

With some regret I went back to England and to the Institute of Education for the Post graduate Certificate in Education course. Every week the Department of Modern Languages shared Methodology in Language Teaching with students from the

Department of Education in Developing Countries. One day a student friend told me: "My tutor, Ken Cripwell, thinks you're wasted teaching French. He thinks, as a nurse, you should be teaching English as a Second Language to health personnel overseas." The feelings I had had in Nigeria about wanting to be part of development crystallised and I went to see Ken Cripwell. Without preamble, I said: "I gather from Gay that you think I'm in the wrong Department." Ken Cripwell didn't bat an eyelid. "If you're Joan Hall, you are." he said and agreed to take me in his group if I fixed it with Modern Languages. A few days later I changed groups - and the whole course of my life. From then on my career was "other-directed". I told Phyllis all about the change and she helped to set up a two-year contract for me at the Institute of Health, Ahmadu Bello University for the following year.

Meanwhile, I enjoyed the year at the Institute of Education more than any other period of study in my life. Gone were the hassles of school vs Children's Home; gone were the almost impossible demands of operating theatre vs Birkbeck College. For the first time in my life I was on a par with all the other students in my group and the work wasn't overly taxing. I bought all the essential books and many of the recommended ones as I had for the Degree Course so my partial sight and slow, difficult reading wasn't such a handicap.

Part of my teaching practice encompassed teaching English to overseas doctors. I found out many of the difficulties involved in teaching and learning English as a Second Language and that helped a lot in the examination as well later.

At the end of the course I got a Distinction in the Written Examination. We knew that very few failed the exam. but that even fewer got distinctions. Phyllis was on leave from Nigeria when the results came through. Lettice Stuart had gone up to London that day and said she would go and look at the lists for me. When she came back and said that I had a Distinction I wouldn't believe her. I had given her the wrong number; she had read the wrong number. "No," said Lettice, "it had your name against it." Then, I thought, it's a computer error. People like me just didn't get Distinctions. A recording error, some sort of error. I rang Ken Cripwell. "People like me don't get Distinctions, Ken, what's happened?" "You got a

Distinction. That's what happened. It does sometimes happen to people like you, Paula. Congratulations." Phyllis had rung all our friends by the time I had confirmed it with Ken. She was so proud of my achievement. This was no "put it in the rubbish bin" attitude. There was warmth and praise. "I always knew you had it in you, Pauletta dear. Well done." I owed so much of the success to Phyllis. She had encouraged me all the way through and I felt strong and cherished.

A two-year contract as Tutor in English and General Studies had been fixed for me in Nigeria and Phyllis and I left together in July. Our first stop was in Denmark to visit Phyllis's friends, all leading anaesthetists and all ex-students of Phyllis's W.H.O. anaesthetics course in Denmark in 1947. I saw the regard and the deep respect which they had for Phyllis and I wondered. How could I ever expect that someone of Phyllis's eminence would want to be my surrogate mother? What a nerve to have even thought it in the first place. We next visited another ex-student from that first batch; another leading anaesthetist. He opened the door and Phyllis said: "This is my adopted daughter, Pauletta." Willy Dam looked at me for a few seconds. Then he said: "I'm disappointed ..." my heart sank. He didn't approve of me. What about Phyllis's other friends? They hadn't said so but ... Willy Dam was laughing. "When we heard you had an adopted daughter we thought she would be black." My happiness at being introduced as Phyllis's "adopted daughter" took over and I basked in the glow of belonging.

We arrived in Nigeria early one morning before it was really light. We flew in through a thunderstorm and I had my first taste of tropical storms. Massive pillars of dense black cloud skirted lakes of fire where the dawn was breaking and I watched, spellbound, as forked lightning shot to earth with awesome speed. I took some photos of this thrilling spectacle, then turned to share it with Phyllis. I stared in amazement. Phyllis sat, bolt upright and in complete silence, eyes tightly shut and face greenish white. It was my first flight through a thunderstorm, leave alone a tropical one, and I had no idea of the mortal danger we were in nor of the consummate skill of the pilot in negotiating it.

Once on the ground my euphoria was swept away. I could see

nothing outside and very little inside. The lights in the hut-like building were so dim that they were useless to me. How was I going to manage in the dark? There were no street lamps or lights from buildings; none of the things which helped me in England.

I had a week to "acclimatise" then work began. The classroom, which was shady and cool, had a thatched roof which was supported by eight stout poles. Unexpected visitors, such as snakes, would slither in from time to time and the whole class would leap to their feet and chase them out again. Such episodes added quite a lot of interest to the working day.

"Situational context" was the new way to teach languages and I used it whenever I could. For example, I was teaching the students how to write ward reports on their patients when an accident happened just outside the classroom. Since the students all rushed outside to get a better look I sent them off to find out about it. When they came back we had a lively half-hour. Two prisoners, first offenders, were hand-cuffed to the handlebars of a policemen's bike. They had been knocked over by a land-rover. "How do you know they're first offenders?" I asked. "Because they are wearing pink stripes. If they go to prison again they will wear blue stripes." "How do you know the land-rover caused the accident?" "Because he had smooth tyres." Gradually we drew a complete picture of the accident and recorded the important features. At the end, I said: "Make a report about your patients like that. Only put in the important things. Then you will write good reports." I had thrown away my prepared notes.

Teaching English for Special Purposes was a very new field in the 1970's and there were no ready-made materials for me so I had to make my own. It was excellent practice and at the end of the two years I learnt what did and didn't work. I also found that writing materials is a highly complex skill and I had learnt something of it during the Postgraduate Certificate in Education course. However, I soon found that I didn't know enough so I wrote to Ken Cripwell to ask his advice. I kept in touch with him and he often gave me help and advice. On this occasion he said that a Master's Degree in Applied Linguistics was a "must". Linguistics is the study of the nature and structure of language; Applied Linguistics is the application of that study to language teaching. Ken added that the Master's at Essex University was the best.

I lived with Phyllis and though we were both working flat out, we made time in the evenings for a short walk up on a nearby rocky hill before the sudden onset of the night. No gentle, lingering dusk this; we had half-an-hour from full daylight to darkness so we made the most of it. We had no housework or gardening to do as all households, Nigerian and ex-patriate, had stewards, garden boys and Toureg night-watchmen. This gave us time to sit over a beer and watch the night.

I soon renewed my acquaintance with Caesar for he still came to the house to enjoy a beer and discuss the latest developments in his and our work. Now that I was fully involved in health care I had more to offer and Caesar sometimes sought my opinion and advice as well as Phyllis's.

Phyllis and I overlapped in Nigeria by six months in 1970 and during that time I made a move I had wanted to make for some time. I had wanted to ask Phyllis if I could take her name but hadn't had the courage to mention it. For weeks I mulled it over. How would Phyllis feel if I suggested it? Would she think I was mentally disturbed? Would she think it was a cheek to want to change my name to hers? Would she think I was making a lot of fuss about nothing? It was by no means nothing to me but would she see it like that? I wanted to leave that armour-plated, hostile orphan behind and tell the world I was a new person; I had a mother.

Eventually I pushed myself far enough to ask her. I had to leave myself enough leeway to back out nonchalantly if she refused; to hide the hurt and the rejection. "Phyllis, could I ask you something?" "Go ahead" said Phyllis, encouragingly. With assumed lightness I asked: "Would you mind if I changed my name to yours? It would make things so much easier." Blah, blah. Practical reasons to make the refusal easier to make and to take - on the surface. I held my breath. "If you'd like to do that I'd be quite happy." Phyllis said, matter-of-factly. "You'd better write to Michael (our solicitor) and ask him how to go about it." As straightforward as that. "Mind you," she continued, "it's much easier to change your surname than your first name - or it used to be. Michael will tell you." I hoped she was wrong. I wanted to be Pauletta Edwards; to make the first name official as well. Most people called me Paula by that time, anyway. I was carried away with the joy, the excitement, the warm glow of pleasure that I felt. I wrote to Michael straightaway and could hardly contain myself as I waited for his reply.

The answer was a Deed Poll, in flowery language and with a big red seal on it. Somehow the red seal gave it all the more weight. Once it was signed and sealed I was officially Pauletta Joan Edwards and, by extension, Phyllis's adopted daughter.

Phylllis wrote to her Danish friend, Margrethe, to tell her of the name-change and Margrethe wrote to me. "Leon Tauman is like your godfather." She said: "He has given you a new name." I had wondered how Phyllis's friends felt about the change of name but they all seemed to welcome me as a member of the family. I wrote to the Taumans to tell them what Margrethe had said. Their letter back was heart-warming and made me feel I was really part of Phyllis's life and circle. Merab wrote: April 21st, 1971: "...we were moved and happy about the decision you had made. And Leon felt he had a little place in the change... we like immensely the new combination Pauletta Joan Edwards.. What a nice thought of Margrethe's! Leon a god-parent!

Leon added: "I shall be proud to be your godfather..."

After the name-change I called Phyllis "my mother" to everyone and this led to an unexpected incident. One day when Phyllis came home from the University she said she had something to tell me. Rather hesitantly she told me that the rumour had gone round that I was her illegitimate daughter. "I'm going home soon so it doesn't matter to me but if you want me to sort it out before I go, I will do." "No," I answered, "I would consider it an honour to be your illegitimate daughter. Leave it." So we did. No malicious gossips could tarnish my happiness.

Phyllis went home in March and I was pleased but surprised that Caesar came as often as before. At first I was a little shy but I had got used to his being there with Phyllis. One day in May he came to take me to see the sunset over the lake. I was half-lying on the couch drinking a tonic water. Caesar got himself a beer and came and sat down beside me. We talked of this and that for a while then, very gently, he put his hand on my stomach. It was electric. I thought I ought to mind, be shocked. I wasn't. "I've loved you for a long time," he said, "You know that, don't you?" We kissed; we caressed; we made love and later we had a quiet supper together. "Love is a many-splendoured thing..." What price Sisters Thelma, Annette and Penelope? What had they known? How could they have wanted to sully such a beautiful, natural thing? There had been no sense of threat, no nameless terror; just a surge of love and pleasurable physical excitement.

By that time I was forty years old. It had been a slow growing of love, the kind which, when it surfaces, you know has been there all the time. Slowly and silently over the last few years, I had shed the fears, the sense of shame, the disgust that the Sisters had instilled into us concerning men and I could now love as I was loved.

The time we had was all too short but we didn't know that then. We never sighed about there being no future in it. We just enjoyed what we had. We loved each other deeply and truly and that was enough. We made love when we could - Caesar was often in England when I returned, to discuss joint projects with ODA or other organisations and there was never any furtiveness or guilt when we made love; it was as natural as saying "hello". Our love had to be a secret from everybody - even from Phyllis. She knew Caesar's wife from her Australian days and she was still in touch. I didn't want to put her in a difficult position when next they saw each other. Nor did we want to hurt anybody.

I applied to the University of Essex and the application form duly arrived. There was a question at the end which asked: "Is there anything else you wish us to know?" I said yes. "If I had done the Degree course on a normal, full-time basis I would probably have got an Upper Second." I gave a very brief résumé as to why I thought that might be possible and sent off the papers. Pure cheek and not necessarily correct but the universities were beginning to turn their noses up at Lower Seconds. It was worth a try. Two years previously I wouldn't have had the nerve but Phyllis was mending my self-esteem little by little and doing wonders for my confidence. Whatever the reason, the University of Essex accepted me.

In August 1972 my contract ended and I went straight home. I had five weeks before the M.A. started and I had a lot to do. More than that, I had been away from Phyllis for ten months and I had still not lost the fear that she might cease to exist.

The Master's course was a year of intensively hard work and at the beginning I thought I wouldn't be able to manage it. When I found that at least half the class felt the same way I felt much better. "Don't worry," said one of our lecturers, "It will all suddenly click and you'll wonder why you thought you had a problem." The "click" happened about a week later for me and I began to enjoy the course. With long hours of study and Phyllis's enthusiasm, encouragement and support I very nearly got a Distinction in the Final Examinations. Phyllis was in Iceland on a World Health Organisation lecture tour so I rang and gave the glad tidings. "Iceland will rejoice for you," she said in her own incomparable fashion.

In March, 1973, towards the end of the Master's course, Phyllis was asked to stand as Borough Councillor but she didn't want to take on anything of that nature. She suggested me instead and, as I always wanted to shine in Phyllis's firmament, I agreed. Besides which, Phyllis is always enthusiastic about new ventures, about everything. She would marvel at the form of a sand-dune in the desert even if she had run out of water. Her enthusiasm is highly infectious and I was carried along on it. Neither of us thought of the problems there might be.

We saw our Head of Department individually at the end of the year and when I saw him he said: "If you intend to set up courses overseas for health personnel you should do a Ph.D. Nurses are the lowest form of animal life in most developing countries and you would just be ignored. If you're DOCTOR Edwards all doors will be open to you. You won't have any difficulty. I'll give you a reference." I took his advice.

I applied for and got a Department of Health and Social Security Research Fellowship - on condition that I was registered at a University as a full-time research student. I went to see my previous Head of Department at the Institute of Education and he said: "Tell them you're registered with us." he said. "What, just like that?" I asked, bemused. It all seemed a bit casual. "Suppose they need confirmation?" "Tell 'em to ring me." He answered. "There won't be a problem. You'll be in my Department."

In January, 1974 I started a three-year Ph.D research Degree on "The Problems of Communication Facing Overseas Nurses in Training in England and Wales."

Over the next two years I would visit forty Schools of Nursing twice each, apart from all the rest of the work involved, and by the end of January all was going well. However, with all the travelling and the long hours of study, I spent very little time at home. There were already signs of trouble but I had no time at all to search out its cause.

One day in June I went to the Professor for a routine supervision. I left him with my head reeling and my knees trembling. "The GMC (General Medical Council) has asked me to find someone to produce a language test for overseas doctors wanting to register here and I've told them you'll do the Listening Test. I've arranged a six-month deferment for you." There wasn't any suggestion that I had any choice. I understood that I was being given a plum but I didn't think that I was fitted for constructing a test for doctors. I didn't say so. I did as I was told, as the Children's Home and nursing had taught me to do.

"What an opportunity," I said, "It will be excellent experience. When do I start?" "In a couple of weeks." said the Professor airily. Changing horses suddenly in midstream was obviously quite normal. I didn't tell him of my panic; nor of all my travelling arrangements to Schools of Nursing; I didn't tell him of my meeting with my second supervisor, the Registrar of the General Nursing Council; nor of the other dozens of appointments already made, all neatly dovetailed throughout England and Wales to save both time and money. None of this could be changed so I did it all at the same time as the Doctors' Test but, to give myself some leeway, I told the GMC that I couldn't start until July 1st. I couldn't attend that first meeting. I had a stomach upset.

The Language Test added even more travelling to an already near-impossible schedule and as my academic and Council commitments increased manifold I had less and less time for just living and enjoying life with Phyllis. The strain on our relationship was immense and was suddenly posing a serious threat to it.

I began to live under the influence of two mounting pressures: a successful academic, her career developing rapidly through other people and all the while feigning confidence, boxing and coxing with a scared child fearful of losing everything, trying to escape and grow up. My sexual maturity with and love for Caesar had no effect at all on my child-feelings, which became stronger as the stresses increased. The vortex, which had begun to spin in 1967 gathered speed and force. It was to spin almost out of control for several years and I was often in danger of being sucked in when the two pressure gauges went high into the red.

Chapter 5

In The Vortex

"... and who gives a child a home
Builds palaces..."

John Masefield, Everlasting Mercy.

Even dashing home whenever I could afford the time and often when I couldn't, I was still away for most of the time. This led Phyllis one day to say that I was more like a lodger than a member of the family. I was staggered and wounded by the criticism but, more, I didn't really understand what she meant. I did as much as I could when I could. Phyllis told me that she was concerned at my "standing aside." Why did I leave her to do all the talking when we had guests? I was all right on actually doing things, she said, but I was no good at drawing out quiet, shy people or helping the conversation along. Part of the answer was that I was too busy being quiet and shy myself. The other part was my inferiority complex about not having anything intelligent to say.

"It's time for you to start helping me to run the household," said Phyllis and suddenly withdrew all help overnight. I was confused and distressed. Phyllis had always run the household ... I rejoined the hedgehogs. This devastating event occurred at the worst possible time, which further distorted my already jaundiced reaction to it. The previous weekend, at the beginning of February, 1975, I had been to stay with Miss Russell and I had asked her to tell me more about my mother. I also told her a lot about the real state of affairs at The Haven. "When you took me there," I told her, "it wasn't so bad. If Mouldy Cheese and Aggy Ragbag had stayed there it might have been all right." I told her about Sisters Thelma, Annette and

Penelope. I finished by saying that Sister Annette was the worst. "She was a real cat and we couldn't trust her an inch." My diary for that weekend says:

"...I told Miss R that Sister (Annette) was a cat and she commented that a friend of hers had said the same. (The friend knew the Sisters and the Convent and Miss Russell gave her name.) She (Miss R) says I'm beginning to look exactly like my mother...and that my mother was vicious and cruel. Miss R tells me I was well out of it. (though the Orphanage was hardly any better.) Perhaps though it's better to be torn apart by strangers than by one's own family but it has certainly left me with scars which I fear will never heal. Poor Phyllis. She finds it hard to understand."

Miss Russell also said that my mother was very violent towards her step-children and that she had often been very cruel to them, actually doing them physical harm.

My father's first wife had died and he took six children to his marriage with my mother. The cruelty and violence weren't born of flashes of anger or exasperation under stress though. They were often deliberate and premeditated and born of innate viciousness. I was profoundly shocked by this talk. Not so much because of what I had learnt that day about my mother. I knew a little of it already and I had had enough experience of deliberate cruelty myself. The talk had underlined and extended my knowledge of the kind and frequency of my mother's particular brand of viciousness. I was disturbed when I thought back to the days of my own violence in the Children's Home. Each instance of it had been an overflowing of the pent-up frustration, despair and misery, like the lancing of a boil. I had never been violent towards anyone since I had left The Haven and I could never hurt a child or an animal. I had bumped Pudding's pushchair up and down kerbs but that wasn't to hurt her and it didn't; it had more effect on me. I had just wanted Pudding to be a baby and not a pudding; to get some kind of reaction out of her. Yet I had deliberately provoked the Sisters at my own expense to try to assuage the fires within me. Was I like my mother? I was deeply troubled.

I had an urgent need to talk all this over with Phyllis but when I got home she faced me with the lodger business and immediately distanced herself from me. No longer did she do odd things for me when Council demands prevented me from doing them and her seeming change in attitude left me very uncertain and tense. I had just been given even more proof of my mother's cruelty and violence, I had an overwhelming dread of what I might have inherited and now Phyllis had withdrawn from me. Each was extremely difficult to handle on its own. All three together were crushing. The child in me took to provoking Phyllis to try to lessen the horror and the hurt but this wasn't the same as goading the Sisters; they would just hit back and award me a bit of respite. I loved Phyllis and when I hurt her - especially when it was calculated - it made the ache in me more acute. I needed more than ever that hug, that reassurance that everything was really all right. Instead, Phyllis's very vulnerability made it all so much worse. As I got more and more irritable Phyllis drew even further away. By the end of February I was being sucked into the funnel of the vortex and it was like waiting for the end of the world. The disintegrative nightmares came much more often: I would be walking along a road and it would suddenly craze, leaving me marooned in the middle; I would be climbing up a staircase on the outside of a house and as I reached the top step the house would crumble away. I was too high up to jump and in danger of falling into the rubble; I would be approaching a hill, ready to go up, and the ground would turn into a bog. There was just enough firm land left for me to stand on. Phyllis would be at the top of the hill and going out of sight. Awake, I was almost never free of the fear of my world crumbling and leaving me with nothing; my fear fed my nightmares and the nightmares stoked my fear. I couldn't stand it any longer.

One morning, conciliatory and trembling inside, I went down to Phyllis. "Phyllis," I asked, "can we talk?" "Yes, if you want to." she answered, but not very welcomingly. This, in itself, was revelatory. "I'm sorry about the last couple of weeks," I began, rather hesitantly. "Yes, well, I think you need to pull yourself together." said Phyllis, walking sideways towards her bedroom. Phyllis would always much rather let the dust settle by itself than explore the reasons why it rose in the first place. I knew that this time it wouldn't settle by itself - if, indeed, it settled at all. Forlorn and in dread I slapped my hand down on the table. "Please, Phyllis, please don't go away. Please come and talk." She came across and sat down at the table. "What's wrong?" I asked, fearful of the answer. To my surprise, for one brief moment Phyllis actually *looked* hurt and vulnerable. We talked for some time; tried to find an answer. "You're getting very secretive, you know." said Phyllis sadly, "You're shutting me out." She said she had stopped "coddling" me because she thought I should have grown out of the need. "I think you ought to go away and sort yourself out," she finished. Oh dear. I knew that I was making Phyllis unhappy and this was a clear invitation to get out of her life. Why couldn't she have told me about the "coddling"? At least I would have known where I was. Why did she always have to button everything up? We had finally brought it all out into the open but it hadn't helped a lot. We had guests for lunch so I had to stifle my feelings and we had a pleasant meal, with smiles and laughter. More importantly, Phyllis and I had a quiet, friendly supper together.

The following day I went to London and stayed at Ethel's flat overnight. I often stayed there, sometimes even when Ethel was away. It might just be that my schedule was too tight to be able to go home; or it might be that I needed time to think but, more and more frequently in the mid-1970s, it was because both the pressure gauges were well into the red. That day, they were both at the point of destructive discharge. I rang Phyllis in the evening. She had had a bad headache so she had stayed in bed all day. She said again that she thought I ought to go away and sort myself out. I was sorely tempted. Perhaps it would be better to go away; leave Phyllis to herself again. Stop making her unhappy and tearing myself to shreds. I obviously couldn't make real relationships.

I should have been working on my thesis that evening. Instead, I knitted furiously as I thought things out. "Through the night of doubt and sorrow" inside me the little girl was trying to grow up. Phyllis and I seemed happy for much of the time and we enjoyed ourselves: the walks and the pleasures of looking for the first signs of change in the season; the fun of identifying birds and flowers which were new to us; the amazement when hundreds of Brent geese came in to land; the thrill of a rare sight of a Great Northern diver; tea in the garden and Mehitabel teaching her kitten to hunt ... How could this all suddenly disappear? Where did disasters like this come from? This was no ordinary disagreement; a chill wind was blowing through our relationship. Even the growing-up child couldn't face the prospect of having to leave home. Home ... I began to cry. Ethel was away that evening. I couldn't watch television but I turned on the radio. A bit of dum-de-dum pop music might help.

> *Got along without you before I met you,*
> *Gonna get along without you now ...*

Oh God! Not that. I turned the radio off and cried in earnest. The next day I went home early and stayed there all day. Phyllis was her usual outgoing self and I felt a little less threatened.

We were peaceable enough together that summer. Our saving grace was always that we didn't quarrel. My anger is the match-flaring kind; over in seconds. Phyllis would withdraw in chilly silence but that never lasted long either. Had they been prolonged there would have been no relationship because both of us are disturbed by quarrelling. Even so, I was often difficult, verging on rudeness, in public. I wanted, needed to be with Phyllis but, when I was, I wasn't always very civil to her. One day, Phyllis said, as we were driving away from a friend's house: "Why did you say that? It's as if you're trying to score off me and I don't think I can stand it any more." On another occasion I had had a sudden flare of anger, born of insecurity and Phyllis was bewildered and confused. "Well, I don't know," she protested, "...just when I think things are going all right, something like this happens." I could never explain those sudden flashes of lightning.

Phyllis didn't often let the "crazy, mixed up kid" get to her but when she did, my spirit quailed. Whenever she retreated in earnest, I was allowed so near but no further. On November 8th, 1975, my diary says:

"... somehow she switches off. What are we to do? We seem to be growing further apart rather than closer ..."

It was Phyllis's reticence about how she felt which I couldn't come to terms with. It was partly that which made me goad her. When Phyllis did go into her shell it was usually without any comment at all and I was left wondering. Unlike Ethel, who chewed me up in her bad moods and that was that, Phyllis never did. She very seldom showed anger with anyone even if she felt it. She certainly never took it out on me but in the mid-1970s she was beginning to feel more than anger towards me. I knew that but because she was closed up I had to try and work out why on my own.

1975 was the worst year in this way for us. By November we were nearly at the end of the road. I was much too heavily overloaded with professional work, Council demands and constituency support to have much time for the most important things of all; learning to live with Phyllis and to grow up; to watch over our relationship and to steer it clear of the rocks. Up in London overnight I would try to sort it all out; find the way to safety through the stormy waters. Was it really so impossible to grow to love and to care properly if you'd never learnt as a child? I'd known Phyllis for fourteen years but I still never seemed to get it right for very long. We were still walking and exploring together but, content though we seemed to be, the happiness was mostly only skin deep. Underneath was a lake of wistfulness and hunger. I did love Phyllis and I cared deeply about her but it didn't seem to be coming across like that. Otherwise she wouldn't be so saddened. I never found an answer in my musings. I only got nearer the centre of the vortex.

In the last few weeks of the year we reached crisis point. I could never work when Phyllis and I were at variance with each other and by the end of the year my work was suffering badly. So was I. I hid my rising alarm and sorrow behind the usual off-hand "so what?", which didn't help at all. My protective shield had large holes in it and was no longer any use. I was emotionally defenceless.

That same year was to lead to the moment of truth for us; Waterloo or Watershed?

Late in October Phyllis went away and she didn't write at all, though she did phone once. This was a warning in itself. When she came home I had a special supper waiting for her but as soon as she arrived disaster struck. Too many things caused disappointment and hurt through misunderstanding and misinterpretation and, instead of our spending a pleasant evening together, Phyllis went to bed early. She was hiding utter dejection under frosty displeasure. I felt forsaken. I was sucked into the vortex and I knew that this time I wouldn't surface again. My silent pool had been turned into a menacing cataract. I couldn't think about the future. I went to bed more alone than I had ever been in my life.

Next day Phyllis said: "We will have to rethink our future together. You obviously aren't happy. Whenever I go away you don't seem to want me home again. We always have trouble." True - but I thought it was her who was out of kilter, like the previous night. I couldn't say anything. I had just been blown apart. I had thought that I had a family, a mother, but - like in The Haven - I had really been on the road to nowhere and now I faced an empty, lonely road ahead.

Up to then, the smallest hiccup, the tiniest furrow in our relationship and I had been ready to fear the worst. Being told now that I had to go was a calamity of limitless proportions. Perhaps I had misunderstood all along. That night I had yet another disintegrative nightmare. I was in a concrete yard with high walls. Suddenly the concrete floor broke up and I fell into a hole. I clutched at the edge as I fell and just managed to hang on but very precariously.

The next day I got up reluctantly and went about my business mechanically. I was beyond being pseudo-nonchalant and offhand. In the depths of the vortex they were useless. As I worked, past thought and sinking lower, a hand reached down and pulled me out. "Let's take a picnic and go to the sea." Phyllis said, "It's such a lovely day and it would be a pity to waste it." As I got ready I wondered. Was there any point? It would soon be all over. Did I really want to be tormented by what might have been? The excitement as Phyllis showed me a nuthatch for the first time; the wind and sun on our faces as we strode along the Essex beaches; the picnics, where the birds sang and the squirrels scampered in the trees?

"Come on," said Phyllis as we walked along the sea's edge. "Tell me what's bothering you." She didn't often start a deep discussion at personal level. I didn't answer; what was there to say? "We can't go on like this." she went on and gradually, slowly, I told her about my fears, my insecurity and now having to go away. "I thought you weren't happy," said Phyllis gently. "I thought it would be better for you to be by yourself. You don't have to go." Between bird-watching and flower-hunting we sorted out many of the causes of our unrest. Then Phyllis said: "I had no idea you felt this way. Whyever didn't you tell me? I could have told you there was nothing to worry about. I just thought that since you're so keyed up at the moment a little time away from it all would give you time to stand and stare. Don't let it build up like this. Do tell me and we'll sort it out in future." We were both much more at ease by the time we got home.

We spent many light-hearted hours together until the 29th November, when Phyllis went to China. I worked at home as much as possible to be with her before she left; Phyllis helped me with curtains in my sitting room, upholstering my settee and we seemed in harmony. There was something, somewhere but I couldn't put my finger on it. I dismissed it and was almost at peace when I saw Phyllis off. She had told me not to write to her in China because they would be moving round too much. At the beginning of December I started a letter to her - a kind of diary. After a week I sent it to Hong Kong so that it would be waiting for her.

Always, when she was away, Phyllis wrote about twice a week. For the first three weeks there was nothing and the niggling "something" which I had discounted came back much more insistently. I pleaded with myself in anguish: "Let me be wrong!" my peace was so frail. Perhaps in China posting letters wasn't very easy ... She didn't have time to write ... Phyllis writes letters while she's waiting for a train. I almost talked myself out of worrying and on December 16th my spirits rose; a letter at last. It was a friendly letter but with a sting in the tail. It referred to something which had happened four weeks previously and should have, would have been trivial had we talked about it then. It no longer was. Four weeks and 6,000 miles had given it status. I thought I would write to Phyllis next day but I couldn't; I didn't know how. I waited until it was easier to handle and even then I avoided the hurting matter. Phyllis's answer to it on December 29th brought up the troubles of November 8th when she had returned from Bath. This raking up of past "wrongdoings" thoroughly demoralised me. Why couldn't Phyllis either sort it out at the time or leave it alone? Hopeless longing welled up in me and robbed me of the will to do anything at all.

It so happened that Caesar came to see me on the same day. He looked closely at me, then wrapped me in a bearhug. "Darling Paula, whatever's the matter?" Dammed-up feelings and tears held back for so long were released in a torrent. Caesar held me, soothed me, quieted me and he stayed for some time, thus easing the pain a trifle. The following week I went to stay with the Heymanns. Desperate and lacklustre as I was, Mrs Haitch and Lotte comforted me with their love and caring. We talked far into the night, which was most unusual, and I felt a fraction better when I left.

Back at home I sat wondering what to do. Should I write or let it all go? If I let it go we would never sort anything out. We were already far into the disaster zone. I was still troubled as to why Phyllis dealt with matters at such a distance of time and space. I knew I had to write, say what was in my heart. If Phyllis didn't respond I would have to go and that would be that.

Late in the evening I started to write. I said it this way, then that way, then I threw it away. Eventually I confronted it squarely. I described the misunderstandings and misinterpretations of November 8th; what we might have said that we didn't; how that might have saved the homecoming from disaster. If she never admitted to being hurt or upset how could I know? If she would never say why it hurt how could I build up a bank of experience for future behaviour?

As I wrote I had a sudden flash of insight - or was it just that I was able to look outwards now and see Phyllis as she really was? Phyllis was as vulnerable as I was and her armour was every bit as thick; except that she had broken through mine. I thought that, somehow, I might be piercing hers; perhaps Phyllis had the same problem as me as to whether to speak or not or, more likely, she fought shy of my ever-ready verbal defence-weapons. Maybe she really believed in the "don't-care-anyway". If I was wrong the price was going to be very high but I knew that I had to take that risk. If we didn't cross this river now, we never would.

I went on writing ... we all need armour but if our armour is too thick it isn't always easy to tell when a hurt had been inflicted, or if the wound is superficial or deep.

"I often don't know what you've thought or how you've interpreted a situation until days, weeks or even months later when you take me completely by surprise by alluding to it in such a way which suggests that at the time you were rankled, surprised, hurt or angered or that you put a completely different interpretation on it than you indicated at the time. This can be very bewildering if not disconcerting...It seems to me that sometimes talking a thing out helps...to crystallise one's thoughts and I always hope that deeper understanding will be achieved by it. Perhaps on the other hand it only serves to confuse... If you see a situation in a particular light then that's how it is - for you. Just as it is for me..."

I received Phyllis's answer to this letter on March 2nd, 1976. She was ready to discuss the issues that I had raised but she seemed to think that I meant sharing our deepest innermost thoughts. That wasn't really what I had in mind and, anyway, neither of us would actually want that. I was encouraged by Phyllis's friendly response, though, so I wrote again. It was important to get it right.

I told Phyllis that I meant, rather, sorting out little day-to-day things, on which deeper things are based. It was better to speak to oil the works or even to speak and seize them up rather than to say nothing. What I hated about "social noises," I went on, was that we go to great lengths to make people we don't give a second thought to feel good but sometimes, where we hold love and deep affection, we don't even try to smooth the path to deeper understanding. That was topsy turvy.

"... 'Hurt', in my vocabulary, means a break in one's emotional equilibrium ... ranging from a flash of irritation to deep despair and sorrow. But what I have been suggesting is not that you bare your soul to me or even remark on a situation if you don't want to ... but that if you choose to keep silent, then forever hold your peace. If you are puzzled, annoyed, disappointed, then say so ... at the time ... don't wait ... If you <u>do</u> try my way you might find that because small misunderstandings don't, from neglect, build into big ones there is less need for minute scrutiny ... If the little things are taken care of and <u>kept</u> little, the deeper things look after themselves..."

I was a fine one to talk. I never told Phyllis whenever the sky fell in on me. I just got irritable and antagonistic. I didn't always tell her about the little things either. Phyllis's bringing her hurts up later and *in absentia* might well have been avoidance of my match-flaring tendencies but these were born of insecurity and fear. Long-distance chiding only increased both.

After this exchange of letters I felt much better. Phyllis said she would try it my way. So it wasn't Waterloo. We hadn't quite reached the Watershed yet either but there was renewed hope.

In April Phyllis came home and there were small signs of a new era. I took care to react less fiercely in situations which I would have resented before; Phyllis was more willing to sort little things out - and we hadn't had the usual kind of friction when she came home.

Shortly after Phyllis's return the Council elections took place and on May 6th I was no longer a Councillor. Those three years of my Councillorship had been one of our major problems. We had had so little time together when trouble arose and we needed to talk it through. Now my evenings were mine again and I could spend more time at home.

Over the next year even more changes took place. I was much less cross-grained and Phyllis became gentler and more tolerant. We were much more in accord and I began to lose my fearfulness. I could once again believe in lasting relationships, happiness and homelife. I could dare to hope that success was possible.

There were also signs of my growing up at last. I began to believe that I could have personal opinions of my own and was beginning to stand my ground. I had argued before but it had been like my tactics in the Children's Home; it had been a means of diffusing the power exerted by the twin pressures in my life. Now I could have properly reasoned discussions with Phyllis without being on the defensive or trying to score off her. The vortex had slowed quite considerably.

By August 1977 the next but, mercifully, the final storm was brewing. Phyllis was again behaving as if she had something on her mind and, again, I had no idea what it was. My confidence and security were like yoyos; both plummeted at the least reverse but took rather more time to climb back up.

Phyllis was having a continual flow of visitors and I had very little time to help. I was paying the price of not having explained my workload to her in terms of time needed. She knew the content well enough but she had no idea of what three entertainment sessions in one week meant. For each dinner, I sat up half the night. For three sessions in a week, I had almost no sleep at all. I got more and more tired and began to go only half prepared to work.

In September 1977 I became involved in a project which was to become far bigger than I or anyone else realised at the time and which banked up the approaching storm-clouds.

1978 was the International Year of the Child and the Institutes of Education and Child Health of the University of London together launched a project called CHILD-to-child. The aim of the Project was to teach older children how to look after their younger siblings and how to recognise early signs of sickness. This would save countless infant lives. Two members of staff from each Institute formed the initial Steering Committee and I was one from Education. Again, it didn't occur to me to say no, even though I was already working eighteen hours a day.

Between September 1977 and April 1978 we had to prepare for an International Workshop followed by an International Conference, with participants ranging from primary school teachers to Ministers of Health and Education, from all over the world.

I used Ethel's flat more and more and as work piled up higher and higher I got increasingly cantankerous with Phyllis. I backslid rapidly and Phyllis must have found me impossible to live with. Half-child, I wanted to be told what to do; half-adult, I resented being "other-directed". When Ethel took a lecturer's post in Sheffield I took over her flat; I needed to be near the Institute in the evenings while we were preparing for the CHILD-to-child Project. Again, I wasn't much help at home.

By the beginning of 1978 we were well into the preparations for the Project and I felt as if I were on a treadmill from which there was no escape. Phyllis rang me almost every evening and stayed with me quite often.

On January 10th I was going home for the weekend and Phyllis, who had stayed the night, drove us home. We had a very pleasant journey and chatted amicably together. My diary for that day says "something not quite right" but I put it down to over-tiredness.

On March 12th Phyllis told me she thought I was still a lodger. I was so distraught that I couldn't even think about it. I felt lost - lonely - nothing.

Diary for March 13th:

"... I'm going to have to think about leaving Phyllis in peace and giving her her life back ... At work there was so much talk of future avenues for me but none of it really mattered ... there was no joy in any of it ... Dean of Faculty of Education in Cardiff wants me to contact him re post in coming academic year ... "Blessed is he who expecteth nothing for he shall not be disappointed."

On March 26th I heard that Caesar was dead; he had been killed in a light plane flying from Sydney to Melbourne. The disbelief, the heartache, the futility drove me almost to the point of collapse but I had to cope with the Workshop pretending that there was nothing wrong. I was emotionally punch-drunk. I couldn't even take two or three days off to confront the tearing, wrenching pain and remorse, the anger and the loss; as our love had been secret so had my grieving to be. Many people round me knew Caesar well and they all kept saying what a loss he would be. I wanted to cry aloud: "He's an even greater loss to me! Shut up, all of you. It's breaking my heart." Never had I been so thankful for the Orphanage training in concealing the most intense suffering under rock-steady composure.

Caesar was a very creative person and he used to tell me how much our love enhanced his creativity. Now there was nothing left. I had lost everything - Caesar, Phyllis, home; all was gone. Work was swamping me and losing its zest. I was back in the dizzily spinning vortex and it wouldn't be long before I drowned. With my protective layer gone and my life scattered in pieces round me I needed time and space to recoup. I would go to Cardiff. That would give me a roost to reassemble my life without anyone close to me. I could do it - couldn't I?

I struggled through the CHILD-to-child Workshop and Conference and on April 20th I went home with an immense sigh of relief. Phyllis met me at the station and took us to tea with Leslie and Kathleen Cross. It would start a weekend of peace and content for Phyllis and me and maybe ... The tea visit put paid to the "maybe". We had actually gone to discuss our problems and seek guidance.

Diary for April 20th 1978:

"It's nearly 20 yrs since I've known her and I still haven't got it right. I didn't find out what was wrong with her today. I seem to be the problem. Not her. Maybe I should tell her about Caesar. Oh God!

I didn't, couldn't do anything that evening. I lay on my bed staring into a black hole. I had yet another disintegrative nightmare but this time I knew it was real.

Shortly after that I told Phyllis that I was going to Cardiff. I didn't get very much response but what was I expecting? Phyllis was pleased for me but there really wasn't much to say. The tragedy of it all was that I ever let Phyllis pull me out of the rubble in the first place. She had cleaned off so much of the dirt; hammered out so many of the dents; mended some of the tears; stuck together a few of the breaks. Most of all, she had patched up my self-esteem. Now those patches were splitting with a horribly final sound. Sister Penelope had been right; you can't make a silk purse out of a sow's ear. My thoughts were chaotic: Give her her life back ... Leave her in peace ... Go back where you belong ... She doesn't want a daughter any more ... You've blown it ... Why didn't she tell me ...? She did, often ... She just wasn't speaking your language ... Or you hers ... I almost *wanted* to go back to the rubble, where no-one cared about anyone and I could get back to my untouchable, sterile state.

On the surface, Phyllis I and enjoyed life, walking, talking, gardening, visiting throughout the long vacation. Life as usual ... I had learnt to play the social game, whatever was going on inside me.

One Sunday Phyllis went to Quaker Meeting and I worked in the garden. We hadn't got much longer together and I was determined to do as much as I could for Phyllis before I went. I kept my thoughts away from the day of departure. I intended to make our last days together pleasant and free from strife. After all, it wasn't Phyllis's fault I had muffed it.

I had lunch ready when Phyllis came back. It was lovely not to be harassed by too much work; to have time to dream ...

Over lunch Phyllis said: "I'll come to Cardiff with you ..." For one microscopic fraction of time all was stilled. Then the yoyos sped up to the top of their strings. With that truly selfless act of total commitment Phyllis had pulled me into full adulthood and at long, long last I believed.

We had reached the Watershed.

Chapter 6

At Last Belonging

I climbed the mountain all alone;
The path was rough, the wind blew chill;
I struggled round unfriendly rocks
To see more boulders still.

My heart grew faint and in despair
I cried aloud. Would no-one hear?
An answering voice: I come! I come!
Rang loudly in my ear.

You took my hand; you raised me up
And led me by a different way;
Now flowers grow beneath my feet
Where once the boulders lay.

Pauletta Edwards.
(Published by: Poetry Now in:
Poems for Mum, 1995,
Ed. Kerrie Pateman)

No-one can get out of the rubble heap by themselves; each one needs some kind of support. The longer a person is in the rubble and the greater the damage done, the stronger the support needed to repair that damage. The "cycle of deprivation" which so many people are destined to repeat shows that not everyone who needs it gets that support. The youngsters who become "juvenile delinquents" are testimony to the number who are condemned to stay in the rubble unless they are rescued by someone with the patience to care. Many are tugged out of the heap but don't get the right sort of caring or enough of it for long enough to get straightened out.

Regrettably, we aren't always ready or able to accept the caring immediately even when it is offered; nor to believe in its reality or genuineness. Why should we be? What preparation have we had? This was the most difficult of all the many hazards I was faced with when Phyllis and I decided to adopt each other. Accordingly, Phyllis often suffered acutely even though she didn't always show it and tried very hard to understand. This setting aside of her own sorrow and confusion - especially during the years when I was too introverted to notice her despondency - did much to help the healing. It stilled my sense of rejection and betrayal, even while neither had in fact occurred. I saw both of these in Phyllis's occasional suggestions that we both took "time out". Her astonishing generosity in coming to Cardiff with me beggars description. It was only when I was writing this book that she told me why. She was waiting, she said, to see if I was ready to stand on my own. When she saw that I wasn't she decided to come too. Such total commitment is very rare but it is what finally saved me. When Phyllis sets her hand to the plough she really does finish the furrow. How could she possibly have imagined that the furrow would be so stony; that the mending and the healing would be so hurtful for both of us or so long-drawn-out? Yet we had chosen to become mother and daughter; we knew each other and we were both expecting it to be a happy relationship. I had no knowledge of the real problems and dangers which lay ahead and Phyllis had no inkling of the minefield through which she was to tread - on occasion with such shattering consequences.

However, with a safety net of happiness, love and laughter we were able, slowly and carefully, to climb over the stumbling blocks. Trial and error on my part and assumption on Phyllis's as to what was causing our heartache gave way to greater shared knowledge and insight. I learnt not to be defensive when problems arose, Phyllis grew readier to talk about them and throughout the years of growth we learned together.

What of all those adopted and fostered children with no previous knowledge of their new parents? I know that considerable effort is put into "matching" child with parents but how much do they know of the turmoil which lies ahead? Some adoptions and fosterings work out very well but often the children are "difficult", to say the least. Sometimes the new parents think that their problem-laden, fractious, "chosen" child should be grateful and happy now that they have a loving home. Why? It is for the parents to build trust, to bear the sorrow of seeming rejection by the child of what is offered, with love, guidance and patience and with never a hint of betrayal. Betrayal and rejection are the greatest fears and both are expected and often seen at every turn. The children need to learn and believe - however long it takes - that neither is going to happen. Then they will be grateful in the true sense of the word, as I was; not automatically as demanded, silently or otherwise.

It took Phyllis twenty years, from 1961-1980, with the help of a great number of people, to repair the extensive damage done to me and for me to learn to trust. Once we got beyond the natural boundaries of a professional relationship and I began to care about Phyllis, she found a sceptical, wary, suspicious viper in her bosom, coiled and ready to strike at the least hint of real or imagined danger.

Throughout the time of healing, especially the years between 1970 and 1980, no-one knew of the dragons I had fought in The Haven or that I was still fighting. All that showed were the battle-scars. The only difference was that the Sisters of Mercy were fair game; by warring with them I could try to fend off the dragons. With Phyllis it was quite another matter. As I grew to love Phyllis, so the dragons became monstrous and chewed me to pieces and my behaviour showed it. When Phyllis got into my still, silent pool and started planting flowers I struggled to keep her out but the little girl wanted, needed to pick large bunches and drink deep of their fragrance. Meanwhile, with love and care, Phyllis almost always put up with the outward signs of my monumental inner struggles. She may not have known their strength but she did know that I needed help.

When I look back on all this I wonder how so much stress and strife could have lain dormant inside me without me or anyone else being aware of it; rather like the way in which seeds of some plants lie, sometimes for years, waiting for a fire to sweep over them before they can sprout and flourish. I wonder, too, how many people who adopt or foster know that the fire must rage if the flowers are to blossom but that the fire must not be stoked or left to burn out of control.

By 1980, little showed of the ravaging destructiveness of my childhood years and Phyllis and I were no longer striving for my deliverance. We were living in peace and tranquility and I really was the composed professional woman I had pretended to be for so long.

In 1987 I became an international health services consultant and looked forward to years of passing on my knowledge and skills to those who needed them most.

First I went to Somalia to help upgrade the tutors' skills in the School of Nursing. Five months into my contract the civil war broke out and, after a week of shelling, shooting and killing, we were pulled out by the United Nations. Phyllis met me at Heathrow and, during the weeks that it took me to recover, she was always there when she was needed. She didn't crowd me or intrude but she listened when I wanted to talk and shielded me from visitors when I wasn't up to seeing them.

One morning I was doing a jigsaw and, quite without warning, the tears of restoration began to flow. I heard a soft "Oh." behind me, then Phyllis on the phone: "I won't be coming to (Quaker) Meeting today. Pauletta needs me." The tears were silent and I had my back to Phyllis so I didn't even know that she had seen. She said nothing but found little jobs to do quietly near at hand for when I was ready to talk.

Five months later I went to Zanzibar as Continuing Education Adviser to the Government. There were never any drugs in the hospital so we gave them on prescription to anyone who needed them for a child.

I had been in Zanzibar for seven weeks when, on January 8th, 1989, two young men came to the house, apparently looking for drugs. What they really wanted was money and we had a safe full of it. They were drug addicts. Violence offered in Zanzibar carries a life sentence - and it *is* life - and I was offered violence of the most bizarre nature. As I could identify the two young men, the house was secluded and there was no-one about, the outcome was predictable. I was left for dead from strangling, chloroforming and severe head injuries. If I have to fight, I'm a "no-holds-barred" fighter, I've discovered, which no doubt foiled the first two attempts. The head injuries were inflicted with a motor-cycle shock absorber, which caused severe concussion. The latter is always followed by a few seconds of not breathing and those few very precious seconds almost certainly saved my life. After four days without medical treatment I was medevacced out, with scarcely any recollection of the four days or the journey.

I do have snapshot memories and my most cherished one is of becoming aware that Phyllis was close at hand. "This is getting a bit monotonous, isn't it?" she said, gently and lovingly. That was at Heathrow airport, I discovered later. All Phyllis's caring, all the changes in me, my love for Phyllis, the warm, strong mother-and-daughter relationship were there in that one moment of clarity. I knew that I was safe; that I was back with Phyllis and everything would be all right. I was still deeply shocked and ill but I didn't realise that. All I knew was that Phyllis was there. What a snapshot. What a mother. Afterwards Phyllis told me that she hadn't recognised me when I came through in a wheelchair. With a neck grossly swollen and finger-marked, cuts all round my mouth from the chloroform phial and a larger-than-life bruised and battered face, that was hardly surprising. As Phyllis passed the wheelchair, looking for me, she suddenly realised that the body in the chair was wearing my clothes. In the snapshot of her greeting there was no hint of the awful shock she must have felt; only the warm, loving welcome home.

From then on Phyllis helped me back to normal. It took seven months for me to learn to walk and talk properly again, to get my co-ordination back and to think straight. In the marathon task of restoring myself to working order, without benefit of medical assistance, Phyllis was a tower of strength. She encouraged me without bullying; praised my puny efforts in order to make me reach further; stood by to give me confidence in case I thought I would fall when I was learning to walk. She listened without complaint to my slurred, monotonous voice as I tried to get my own voice back.

Seven long months later, gruelling for both of us, I was normal enough on the surface to go back to work.

Twice I went back, for three and a half months each time, but right from the start I had lived on a roller-coaster of vertigo and imbalance and there were too many left-overs from the attack to make work feasible so, sadly, at the age of 55, I had to give up work altogether. With an increasing muscular disorder and some of the effects of the head injuries being permanent, Phyllis and I have had yet more learning to do. Phyllis is now in her mid-80's and we should be gradually reversing roles. We can't do this to any great extent because I am quite disabled but we have worked everything out so that my limitations aren't very obvious to others.

The effects of head injuries often lead to the break-up of relationships and great trouble in families. Since the relationship between Phyllis and I had already been tried and tested to the utmost limit over several decades it stood up to the early strains. When it became apparent that some of the effects weren't going to go away we took them in our stride and adapted to them.

In the early days of our relationship I had been afraid of being left, defences half-demolished, to fend for myself again emotionally but Phyllis was loyal and she was steadfast; she was ready to wait, to help, to hold me up against considerable cantankerousness, until I could stand by myself. After the attack she had to do the same thing but this time with my co-operation. This time there was not the wearing, tearing, emotional dependence of the little girl or the not believing and not trusting of the 1970s. It has been more a decreasing physical dependency and though, with Phyllis's help, I have made great strides I will never quite stand by myself again in this respect.

Fortunately, the psychological effects of being nearly murdered were short-lived. With the emotional dragons I had had to fight for so long before and after I met Phyllis, I had weapons and experience enough to slay almost immediately the relatively minor ones which followed the attack.

I used to be very athletic and after the attack there were times when the loss of physical prowess was extremely frustrating. Coming to terms with the problems associated with radical changes in my life was sometimes daunting but I talked it all over with Phyllis without making too big a thing of it. Phyllis had taught me in our most fraught years that not releasing the safety valves only increased the tension to danger-level. I should know.

As I had grown more trusting I had been more and more able to tell Phyllis why I felt this or that way. Phyllis had shown me that often I was over-reacting and getting things out of proportion. In this way we had reached the Watershed. By the same token, in defusing the tensions of post-attack living before they got too high I was able to keep things in proper perspective and that greatly helped my recovery. It was sometimes very tough for both of us but we had been there before so we knew the way out.

Not all that happened to me or that I learnt has been as helpful. Some marks of the stormy days are still apparent. When Phyllis fished me out of the rubble and stuck the pieces together she eradicated most of the effects of my savage past but however carefully and patiently something is mended, traces of the damage will always show.

I am no longer the "cat walking by his wild lone but never telling nobody". There is nothing of those ferocious undercurrents left and I have a deep inner peace which not many people achieve. Inner peace though, is usually associated with a quiet, gentle voice but I apparently often sound aggressive even when I'm feeling very benign. I am quite hurt when I'm asked why I'm cross when I'm not. Evidently, the weapons of defence aren't always laid aside with the reasons for their need.

By turning into a little girl and going through that stage of emotional development as an adult, I thought it was just me that was odd. It seems not. I left that child behind a long time ago but there are apparently several people about who haven't. How many? Two people have asked me what they should do about young women who seem to be in the state I was in. Unlike me, these young women didn't bury it deep and seek their own salvation. They actively sought the hugs and kisses that they so badly needed - from older women. Without any prior knowledge or explanations, this led to serious misunderstanding and the young women lost what they yearned for so much. Both were married so it does seem as if sexual love doesn't block out the "little girl's" needs. Maybe people having that kind of need can't talk about it. I certainly couldn't. Maybe they don't understand it. I didn't really, at the time, either. Nor have I ever heard the "becoming a child" idea aired before - not as a genuine, years-long emotional state. That's why, until my two friends asked my opinion, I thought it was my particular kink.

I have one trait which I thought I had left behind with the little girl but I fear I haven't. I was telling Phyllis about Ethel saying that, in my youth, when I was with someone I was very much with them but when they were gone they ceased to exist for me. "You're still a bit like that." said Phyllis. I asked if, perhaps, it wasn't one of the effects of the head injuries. "Not really," she answered, "You were like it before you were hit on the head." Oh dear. I don't really want to believe that - but, then, there's a lot in this book I would rather not believe.

There is one strand of the legacy of my past which I do admit to. I resent authority in any shape or form. I hate to be organised and I take unreasonable exception when I am. I have never liked being "other-directed" and I don't mellow with age.

Probably dating back to the same period of indoctrination is my fear of losing approval points. This is partly the reason why I was always afraid of people, especially friends. Phyllis still chides me sometimes for taking criticism as a personal attack. With her I do, though we both now know that it is an automatic response which no longer has any real meaning.

Many of the areas where I haven't really recovered are to do with fear. In The Haven and at school I was dominated by fear. In nursing there were anxieties of another kind. From the time I met Phyllis until we reached the Watershed there was an all-pervading dread of a highly complex nature. What puzzles me most is how none of these fears were noticeable. Certainly while I was "climbing the ladder" everyone saw only a successful professional woman - not a terrified adult-child stuck on with BluTak. The Haven had taught me so well how to disguise my feelings and no-one, not even Phyllis, would know them now if I didn't have a purpose for writing this book.

Talking of Phyllis, I have - or would have if I gave it house room

- a more-than-normal apprehension whenever she is away. It dates back to the days when I was afraid that she would vanish like the mother of my nightmare. The feeling has nothing to do with accidents or heart attacks. It is much more nebulous. Even though firmly sat upon it is still there if I let it in.

I realise that these are all inappropriate responses, no longer wanted on voyage, so I stifle or dismiss them whenever possible. I don't let them impinge on life or give voice to them if I can help it but sometimes I can't stop it. For example, take being stroppy or bellicose. These were weapons for forty-six years so they aren't easily silenced. In fact, I still use being stroppy as a weapon. If I am hurt or uncertain, I hide it, as I used to and the stroppier I am the more I am hiding. This habit seems to be too ingrained to change.

Even though Phyllis could not erase all the effects she has done a remarkable job in taking into her life a wary and doubting, sometimes withdrawn individual along with the frightened child and turning her into a reasonably sociable adult. It took me a long time to learn, even longer to believe that Phyllis loved and cared for me as a daughter. This, in spite of the countless ways in which she showed it - but with her help and patience I did learn. We both did.

As Matthew Arnold says: "... chance will see us through ..."

How little I knew just how far the "chance" of going back to Harrow Hospital and meeting Dr Edwards was to bring me through. At the time, I didn't even know how far I had to come, nor how long the journey would be.

In 1993 I wrote a poem as a tribute to Phyllis and I gave it to her on Mother's Day, March 21st, 1993:

TO PHYLLIS

I love you for your strength
Your serenity and peace
Which give me strength;
Your spirit, independent
And unhampered by what
Others think about you;
Your capacity for making
Friends and keeping them;
Your mind, so quick to grasp
And analyse, untrammelled
By too great a weight
Of narrow expertise,
Roaming at ease across
So many disciplines;
Your urge to teach and
To pass this knowledge on.
The two who bore and cast
Me off will never know
How great that act which
Left me free to call you
Mother

Pauletta Edwards
in: *Circles in The Sand*, 1995
Ed. Glenn Jones, Published by Anchor Books.